BY NICK TAYLOR

Bass Wars: A Story of Fishing Fame and Fortune
Sins of the Father: The True Story of a Family Running from the Mob
Ordinary Miracles: Life in a Small Church
A Necessary End

A NECESSARY END

NICK TAYLOR

A
Necessary
End

NAN A. TALESE

DOUBLEDAY

New York London Toronto Sydney Auckland

PUBLISHED BY NAN A. TALESE
an imprint of Doubleday, a division of
Bantam Doubleday Dell Publishing Group, Inc.
1540 Broadway, New York, New York 10036

D O U B L E D A Y *is a trademark of*
Doubleday, a division of Bantam
Doubleday Dell Publishing Group, Inc.

Book design by Marysarah Quinn

Original woodcuts by John Taylor

Library of Congress Cataloging-in-Publication Data
Taylor, Nick, 1945–
A necessary end / Nick Taylor. — 1st ed.
p.   cm.
1. Taylor, Nick, 1945–   —Family. 2. Taylor family. 3. United States—
Biography. 4. Death—Social aspects—United States.
I. Title.
CT275.T359A3   1993
929′.2′0973—dc20   *93-14474*
CIP

ISBN 0-385-47102-5

All Rights Reserved
Printed in the United States of America
March 1994

1   3   5   7   9   10   8   6   4   2

First Edition

For Mom and Dad, of course;

For Harley Jones, who was also a good son;

And for my nephew, Doug Tudanger,
his parents, and the rest of my new family.

Of all the wonders that I yet have heard,
It seems to me most strange the men should fear;
Seeing that death, a necessary end,
Will come when it will come.

—from *Julius Caesar,* by William Shakespeare

1983

My mother wrote her own obituary, and my father's, too. I opened one of her letters in May of 1983 expecting the usual news of friends and family, the weather and what she'd been reading lately. Instead, I read: "Clare Unger Taylor died . . ." A space followed, implying that I should add the circumstances. The notice continued with a modest, straightforward description of her life, a gentle life of mild accomplishment. She had done the same with my father: "John Puleston Wotton (Jack) Taylor died . . ."

They died within months of each other some time later, and I took the obituaries out and added what was needed and sent them to the papers she had listed. Still later, I scattered my par-

I

ents' ashes on the sea. But I return often to the time those obituaries introduced, for what I learned of death and life, and continuity, the unending flow of one into the other. It was a period of eight years.

My parents were then in their mid-seventies. My mother was short in stature and nearsighted, and sweet-tempered despite the appearance of a pugnacious chin that quivered when she set her jaw. She had a university degree, from Michigan, and had worked as a reporter, but the thing she was most proud of, other than me and helping to start two libraries, was that she was the first woman who dared to wear pants in the stuffy expatriate community of the small Mexican town where they lived in retirement for several years. "Jocotepec has never been the same," she liked to say. I always thought my mother was born before her time. My father, on the other hand, was born too late. He was a Victorian at heart, in love with order, blind to his own quirks but quick to censure others. He was compact and sinewy, bawdy and ill-tempered. He could roar with laughter and the next minute turn to fierce, protective anger.

He worked as a land surveyor and a draftsman, but I considered his true calling the delicate wood-block prints he made and the sailboat he built from plans he drew himself. I was thirty-seven. I was their only child.

They lived that year in a small town, Waynesville, that lies between the Smoky Mountains and the Blue Ridge in western North Carolina. They had lived there when I was born and moved several times, always to return. This time their home was in a high-rise for the elderly. The building was new and made of sturdy red bricks, and the politicians had gotten up on a flatbed truck and dedicated it with speeches about the time my parents moved in early in the year. Their apartment was on the fifth floor. From the living room's one wide window you could see, across the street, a large maple tree that turned flame red in autumn and a church ground bordered by a low stone wall. The wall made me think about appendicitis. I had been a first grader when a burning stomachache forced me to leave school to meet my mother at a doctor's office. I had gotten as far as the wall, where Mom found me, hugging my knees in pain, and hours later my appendix was removed. That was in 1952.

They took a Florida vacation in 1953, and Mom fell in love with Fort Myers Beach, a resort island and shrimping port on the lower Gulf Coast. We moved that fall, when I was seven, and I grew up and finished high school there. They returned to North Carolina after I finished college, in 1967. They stayed five years, then moved to the Mexican village of Jocotepec, near Guadalajara, in 1972. Four years later they moved back to southwest Florida and into their first high-rise for the elderly, a building on the Caloosahatchee River in Fort Myers called the Presbyterian Apartments. I thought they would stay there. Dad was seventy then, and Mom was sixty-seven. But the restlessness set in after seven years. They decided to return again to North Carolina, and moved just a few months before I opened the mail to find that Mom had written their obituaries.

Waynesville, like everyplace, had changed. The Mount Olive Baptist Church didn't hold its Sunday dinners anymore. The whole town had spread outward to the bypass, and the welcoming "Gateway to the Smokies" sign that once hung

4

over Main Street had been taken down. The downtown newsstand now sold the *New York Times* on Sundays. It was a convenient four-hour drive from my home in Atlanta to Waynesville. Now, after all their moving, surely my parents would stay until they died.

1984

The new year was barely underway when I was helping them pack to return to Mexico. I was against the move. Dad took digitalis for his heart, and Mom wasn't what she used to be. She'd had an accident a few months earlier, and although she'd been indignant when the judge sent her to driving school, it had clearly been her fault. They were determined to go regardless.

A light rain was falling that February morning, increasing my sense of gloomy foreboding. In winter the southern mountains are impassive, as if they've turned their backs and don't give a damn; I felt their rejection in my mood. My wife, Barbara, and I carried suitcases and boxes from their apartment to their big old Plymouth. A row of old men and women sat watching in the lobby, country people who had their own reasons for resenting the circumstances in which they found themselves. They had been corralled from farms and cabins by well-meaning children like myself who came gravely every Sunday to take them out to dinner. Snuff bulged their lips and the women's stockings were rolled down around their calves and they stared at us with the flinty, unforgiving eyes of prisoners watching an escape. They planned to die there; why should anyone be allowed to leave alive? My heart should have soared, but I was thinking of myself.

My parents had been a big part of my life when I was growing up; that is to say, our relationship was necessary. We were not the kind of family that played touch football or went to reunions or even embraced each other heartily. Partly, I think, it was because we were rootless. My father was born in England, my mother on the Upper Peninsula of Michigan. I had an uncle I wouldn't have recognized and cousins I had never met. I went to work after college, lived in three cities in four years, got married, settled in Atlanta, divorced, remarried. Over time I grew used to loving my parents coolly, with a minimum of muss and fuss. I thought it was inconsiderate of them to move to Mexico at their age, when I was beginning to worry about them. It would have been much easier on me if, like the others, they had chosen to simply sit and wait for death.

At last the car was loaded. We stood together in the parking lot, awkward at the moment of departure. Dad was hopping from foot to foot, anxious to get started. Mom had a pained wistfulness in her blue eyes, a look of endurance. I brushed my pursed lips against my mother's lips. I hugged my father, felt him hang on a second longer than we were accustomed to. The forces arrayed against them, these two people who had gotten old, seemed dangerously potent all at once. Mom settled behind the steering wheel. The car engulfed her. She had to tilt her head back to see down the long hood, which raised her chin and emphasized it. Dad wouldn't drive. I couldn't remember the last time he had driven. "Too goddamned much trouble," he said. "Your mother's a good driver, let her drive." He didn't even have a license anymore; he had let it lapse as a way of denying the state's power over him. He took the passenger seat and right away set about fussing. He would have preferred to fly ahead while I drove Mom to Mexico, as he had the last time while we slogged it, but this was my punishment for his insistence. You play, you pay; you want to move to Mexico, you by God don't take the easy way of getting there while your family does the dirty work. I eyed him sitting there and felt some satisfaction at the fifteen hundred miles ahead of him. Serves you right, you mean old fart, I thought. He'd found the short trip to my wedding in Atlanta too much for him the year before. Then he turned a sweet smile upon me. "Goodbye, Nick," he said, and patted my hand resting on the door.

"Come on, Mammy," he said sharply, turning to my mother. "Let's get this show on the road."

"You settle down," she said.

Then my wife and I watched them pull away. I knew as the rain erased their tire tracks that I could not take their safe journey for granted. My concerns were theirs, twenty years removed. Would they be safe? Would they get lost, run out of gas, have a flat tire, fall asleep at the wheel, be run off the road by a drunk? My waking nightmares were lurid and extravagant. The phone would ring in the middle of the night. A sheriff from south Texas would drawl devastating news. I would make a hasty trip to nowhere. We would return on a medevac plane. The inconvenience of it! The expense!

I followed their progress on *National Geographic* maps. They called from Houston and again from Brownsville. When they called from Chapala to say they'd arrived, I felt the relief of a parent whose child reaches home overdue, but safely, from a date. I felt another kind of relief as well, that of lifted responsibility. I could get on with my life.

Their first letters came from a different place from the one-bedroom apartments in the highrises in which they'd lived for several years. My father revealed an amiability with his surroundings he hadn't shown in some time. "We have been in our casita a week and still are unpacking the car," he wrote.

Today Mamacita is off to a garden club luncheon or something. Two gardeners are sprucing up the white geraniums and stuff along one side of the house. They are part of the staff.

Needless to say our quarters are somewhat larger than Waynesville. In the bedroom, besides the two beds, are two armchairs, two upholstered chairs, two dressers and a fireplace! Then there is an adjacent dressing room with closets all along one wall that opens into the bathroom with tiled shower and tiled washbasin and tiled counter on two sides, very attractive. Whereas we have had hardly more than three places to sit down in our apartments, we now have four in the bedroom alone, then five easy chairs and a settee around the fireplace in the living area and a settee, chaise, five chairs and a couple of tables on the porch!! There is still the dining area and kitchen and the extra bedroom and bathroom. It will take a little time to get used to all this space, but it is just great to step out the door onto terra firma, and grass and such. At night the stars are really bright and they seem countless.

"Your room is ready for you at any time," he reminded me in closing.

His letters continued in an expansive vein.

"We are enjoying our casita and the environment more every day," he wrote two weeks later. "The lack of noise is wonderful! The abundance of blooming flowers and the riot of colors is a constant joy, as are the many varieties of new birds and their brilliant plumage. From our dining table we look out over lawn, trees, shrubs—every prospect pleases. Our days are taken as they come." He closed with innocent conviction: "I do not think we need to move again, ever!"

Their weeks in Chapala became months. Dad wrote that he was bringing out his carving tools and ink rollers from the cardboard boxes where he'd stored them in the apartment years, when he'd had no room to use them. He was thinking of making prints again. In the meantime he was designing a bookcase for their bedroom. Mom took on English students, tutoring for free a child of their twice-a-week maid, the maid's younger sister and her boyfriend, and later a couple who had a stall in Chapala's market and wanted to deal better with their English-speaking customers. My parents grumbled that their Social Security checks were slow to find them at their new address. But for the most part, their letters were giddy with delight. They had grasped the life I would have denied them in the interest of my own convenience.

They kept urging me to visit. They fantasized about it, conjuring a "feeling that you might show up any day," as Dad put it in one of his letters, to which he appended directions from the airport. I kept writing back that I had things to do. Mexico was a trip, and as long as things were fine with them, I couldn't spare the time or money. Then Barbara accepted a job with WCBS-TV, and we moved from Atlanta to New York City. It was the next spring before I got around to visiting my parents.

1985

March brought an urgent letter from my mother: "It seems years—centuries—since we have seen you and we have much to discuss, papers for you to sign, etc., important matters that must be dealt with before we follow Wint on the upward? trail. I think your papa was greatly shocked by Wint's sudden demise and has decided that time is of the essence."

Winston McConnell was an old friend. He and his wife and three sons had been our neighbors in Florida when I was growing up. Wint had frolicked scandalously in his last years, when his wife, in a nursing home with Alzheimer's disease, had forgotten who he was. He and his "nurse-companion" descended on my parents in Febru-

ary, but departed suddenly when he got sick. He died soon afterward.

I arrived in Guadalajara on April 17, Mom's seventy-sixth birthday. From the airport's international luggage bay, I saw her waiting outside customs. In the line where I stood, an inspector ordered a nervous campesino to reveal the contents of a gigantic duffel bag. The bag shrank as the man pulled out wads of clothing until, somewhere in the middle, a television set appeared. The campesino turned from the customs man to his family and shrugged helplessly, palms up. The inspector grinned. Beyond him, Mom had seen me and was waving avidly. I passed through customs without an inspection, walked around the long, low wall that separated us, and, for the first time in over a year, hugged her.

"Boy, kiddo, you sure are a sight for sore eyes," she said after we broke apart and she held me at arm's length, viewing me through tears.

"Happy birthday, Mom," I said.

"Oh, that." She waved a hand.

Just then my father came into view, walking with his familiar rolling limp. He hadn't walked till he was five years old. Then his mother died, and with her, her fanatical opposition to the surgery that then repaired his congenitally dislocated hip. The roll had grown more pronounced as he got older, giving the impression that he was walking uphill into a stiff wind. He drew close, broke into a grin, gave me a hug, and took my suitcase, loaded with gifts. The three of us walked into the afternoon heat. At the curb, Dad put the suitcase down, shook his hand, and blew his cheeks out in a long breath. "Heavy," he said. "What have you got in there, bricks?" He let me take it as we crossed the road. In the parking lot, he turned one way, Mom another. He said, "The car's over here." She said, "No, Jack, it's over here." They went off in opposite directions. I jumped up and down and tried to spot the car. Among us it was found and we began the thirty-minute drive to Chapala.

I drove; Dad sat in the front seat and Mom in back. We rode in silence much of the way. Dad denied it, but he had needed a hearing aid for several years. When I tried to talk to Mom, I found myself repeating everything for Dad. But the silence felt comfortable, because my parents were content in my presence and somehow reassured. Outside the windows, the terrain of the Mexican plateau signified the remove at which I found them. It was harsh, uninviting, and chaotic, while I wanted neat, orderly, predictable. The edges of the road—a divided, shoulderless four-lane that swerved abruptly back into a single roadway—dwindled into scrub brush and rocks. Here and there a side road meandered toward a town placed seemingly at random, a cluster of trees and buildings dominated by a church spire. Nothing illustrated quite so well their adventure of foolhardiness and faith, their vulnerability.

The road curved up to a pass in the hills and then fell toward Chapala. The blue lake, also named Chapala, stretched out of sight in either direction. White houses with tile roofs sprinkled the hillsides. A frieze of mountains rose beyond the lake's far shore. Mom had been dozing. Her head shot up abruptly and they both grew animated as they directed me into the town. We turned off the road across from a small bullring and a soccer field and went down a rough cobbled street among a community of houses and storefront cantinas, past a school to a mustard-colored adobe wall with a steel gate in the middle. Dad opened the gate and I drove inside.

I saw immediately what had animated their letters with such pleasure. We were at the back of a lot that was perhaps three quarters of an acre, twice as deep as it was wide, with manicured grass, trimmed shrubbery, and bursting flower beds, shaded by a few large trees and cascading trellises of bougainvillea. Half a dozen one- and two-story houses, all in the mustard adobe of the wall, were arranged behind a big house that occupied a front corner of the lot. A gardener was hoeing weeds from a round flower bed. "Mi hijo," my mother called proudly. "My son." The gardener smiled and lifted his sombrero.

Their house had large arched windows on two sides and a tiled roof rising to a central peak. "It used to be a swan house," Dad said as he opened the door. A door to the left off the wide screened porch led to their suite. Straight ahead beyond a glass door and more arched windows, the main part of the house contained the living room and dining area, a cozy den with fireplace, a small bedroom and a bathroom, all under the exposed

20

roof tiles held up by beams that fanned like spokes out from the central supporting pillar. The kitchen was beyond this at the back.

They were content for the few days of my visit just to have me near them, under their roof again, repeating old patterns. We didn't do much. Each morning my father would pad into the kitchen in his ancient bathrobe to feed the cat and light the burner under the coffee water. Then he would retreat to shave and dress. When he appeared again, in the well-worn khaki slacks and sport shirt that made up his standard uniform, he would put bread in the toaster. Then Mom, in pants and a top and, more often than not as she grew older, a light sweater, would arrive and begin her duties, cooking their soft-boiled eggs for three minutes according to a kitchen timer and cutting the grapefruit. They had followed this routine for years. I could watch them and remember that our house was the only one, when I was growing up, where a father was present in the kitchen. He would stand beside the sink with his sleeves rolled up, drying dishes and sometimes tormenting my mother with a well-placed pinch while she was helpless with her hands in soapy water.

We ate at a table next to one of the arched windows that looked into the garden. A border filled with geraniums and lilies ran alongside the house. Dad had restored a neglected birdbath in the garden. He filled it every morning and watched it from his seat at the table, where he kept his *Field Guide to the Birds* beside his daily regimen of pills. Mom, delegated by the landlady to cut the roses, took them around in a basket to the other tenants and always kept her vases full. When the breakfast dishes were washed and stacked, the remainder of the morning was given to reading, correspondence, and just fiddling. Then we were off to town for the paper, the mail, and the marketing, or lunch if no one felt like cooking.

Chapala had a lush, romantic seediness. There was a tourist market at one end of the town where you could buy huaraches and wall rugs, and a fancy hot spring at the other where you could loll in steaming water drinking margaritas. The lake had receded so that the town pier barely reached the water and goats grazed in the grass that had sprouted in the silt below the beach. Squatters lounged in the yard of the magnificent old train station and hung their drying laundry from its terraces and open windows. It was a life on the verges, somewhere between Graham Greene and Evelyn Waugh, and it was easy not to think about the future as we dwelt in its slow turn. Most nights, my parents tucked in early after a light supper while I sought out the drinking neighbors who had tales to tell.

The day before I was to leave, my mother called me into their bedroom. She was seated at her desk, where another arched window overlooked a different section of the garden. She looked familiar at the desk. Her Royal portable, a dictionary, a glass full of pencils, stacks of cards and letters to be answered, were ranged in front of her, and I saw her as she was when we lived on Florida's Gulf Coast and she was a correspondent for the *Fort Myers News-Press*, writing about big fish and visiting yachtsmen and whatever else she could find to say about the islands she covered— Fort Myers Beach, where we lived, and Sanibel and Captiva—typing on the back of wire service copy and earning a grand fifteen cents a column inch for what the paper printed. I sat on the edge of her bed. She scooted her chair around to face me, wearing the same determined look I'd seen her wear when she was on a deadline, the look that set her chin in the smooth roundness of a river stone, and said, "You know, your father and I aren't going to be around forever."

"I know, Mom," I said.

"I've updated our obituaries." She fished in a manila folder and handed me three sheets of paper. The third was a set of instructions. "Be sure to check on survivors," she had written. Her brother—my Uncle Jack, the uncle I wouldn't have recognized—had lost his feet to diabetes, and her two sisters, my Aunt Dolly and Aunt Marpy, both were older. She wanted an accurate obit, but she must also have been wondering who would outlive whom.

She next produced from the folder several bank cards and gave them to me to sign. "Just in case," she said. This was simple prudence. As a codepositor, I would be able to handle their accounts if they couldn't. It also would obviate inheritance taxes, since the amounts involved fell within the allowable range for gifts. She already had told me in a letter that I was the executor of "the estate." I took her quotation marks as irony;

the estate was so small, only a few thousand dollars, that not even one of Elmore Leonard's characters would have tried to figure out a way to steal it.

I signed the cards and folded the obituaries, but Mom had more papers in her folder. These announced their membership in the Guadalajara Memorial Society. I read the mimeographed information sheet. It said, "In spite of our wonderful climate people do die. This can present problems for your survivors." Bold-faced instructions followed: In case of death, "DO NOT CALL THE POLICE!"

The idea apparently was to prevent property from being confiscated. "Get money out of bank. Tell no one," Mom had written on a separate sheet summarizing all of her instructions. She had added the name of a funeral home and the terse directive, "Tell want cremation—disposal of ashes."

Finally, she handed me a list of their possessions in the house, separate from what the landlady had furnished. It was two and a half pages of items that were mostly small and insignificant— "I flyswatter," "6 Christmas cocktail napkins,"

"3 satin pillowcases." I wondered if in toting up these abraded shreds of life my mother had seen how little she and my father had brought this far. More was in storage back in North Carolina. My legacy of odds and ends.

"Well, I guess that's everything," she said. She sat back with a look of relief and her face softened; her jaw unclenched, and her chin eased from its forward jut. She looked pensive for a moment, fingering her necklace of dried and lacquered seeds. "Nobody likes to talk about these things, you know. But you have to. Your father and I will feel a lot better now that all this is taken care of. We're ready to go to the happy hunting ground."

"I don't think you're ready for that yet," I protested.

"You never know," she said.

A day later, the papers she'd given me folded in my suitcase, I caught my plane for home. If my parents died in spite of Chapala's balmy weather, I had been prepared.

I had no idea.

. . .

It all matters so little now, in retrospect. But at the time, these details seemed to pile complication on top of complication. The folder that contained my parents' obituaries and living wills and items of property and things to do IN CASE OF DEATH, as Mom had labeled one of her pages of instructions, lurked in a file cabinet with its cargo of demands. Death itself was not the problem. The "passage toward deth is more harde and paynfull than dethe it self," Phedrus tells his friend Mercolphus in Erasmus's colloquy on death. Nothing about that has changed in the nearly five hundred years since it was written, except that people are living twice as long. It was my parents' dotage that I feared. I feared their faltering, their decline, and, finally, their dependence. And I could not, as Phedrus advised Mercolphus, cast the "ferefulnesse" of it from my mind.

This was not just my problem. My parents and I were among legions. We would still be among legions today, and tomorrow, and for years to come. People are living twenty years longer than they did in 1920. There are more than thirty-one million people sixty-five and over in the United States, ten times as many as at the turn of the century. Ten million seventy-five and over. Three million eighty-five and over. Most of them are the parents of most of the rest of us, especially the bulge of mid-twenty- to mid-forty-year-olds, of whom there are more than eighty million, more than the population of united Germany. Ours is the tale of the end of the century, not only in the United States but in Canada and Western Europe and Japan, and anywhere children in the bloom of their lives must confront their parents' withering. What do our parents need? What must we do for them? What becomes of us in the process, of our minds and lives and dreams?

I was pondering these things even before I went to Mexico to see my parents. Flying from Guadalajara back to New York, I could not say I'd seen anything to heighten my anxiety. Mom sometimes complained of arthritis. A hiatal hernia, in which the stomach intrudes into the esophagus above the diaphragm—normal in old age, according to one medical text—caused nausea if she ate spicy foods. Her face hurt in cold weather, and her blood pressure was high. My father, now seventy-nine, continued on his digitalis and denied he couldn't hear. Mild skin cancers mottled his high forehead below a head of black hair in which only flecks of gray intruded. If my parents had some minor ailments, they still were living as they wished.

Back in New York, I reckoned my new status as their codepositor invited participation in their business matters. I told Dad I could make more on his investments. This drew Mom's chastising letter:

> Your father prefers to leave everything as is as long as we are living outside the U.S. of A. He says the additional amount of interest is not worth the possible chance of upsetting computers.
>
> Furthermore, he wants all correspondence pertaining to these accounts to be mailed to us until, and if, the time comes when we are no longer able to handle our own business.
>
> You are not to be upset by this but rather, should be grateful that your parents are still

able to do this in a lucid and businesslike fashion. I would say we still have a few years to go before we reach the stage that Marty, at eighty-four, has reached where she can remember her childhood and first marriage down to the last detail but couldn't tell you what happened five minutes ago. Then, we will be glad to have you take over and that should be good news to you at this time.

Marty was their landlady. I had met her when I was in Chapala. She was a leathery old thing who lived alone in the big house in the garden among massifs of Spanish furniture, watched over by the portrait of her dark-eyed first husband in dashing regimentals. She had embraced the prerogatives of age, showing the door to her bewildered second husband when she was eighty-three. She kept a sign on her door telling visitors to go away during her siesta time.

I stopped asking for control of their affairs. Yet I wondered how much longer they would be able to go on. I expected at some point to have to intervene, and I feared for the integrity of my own life. For several months, in fact, I had been massaging my anticipation into an article for *Esquire.* Only part of my concern was contained in Thomas Mann's phrase "A man's dying is more the survivors' affair than his own." I also was trying to fathom my helplessness and confusion at their aging.

The article appeared to reaction that was largely positive. Readers wrote to say that it had expressed their own concerns for their parents and themselves. I learned that many men and women my age were facing what I faced, and shared my fears.

A postcard had arrived from France that summer. The picture was of an empty chair on the beach at St. Tropez. The message was from Jeff Shear, a writer friend, and his wife, Bonnie Cutler, and Jeff told me later the picture was intentionally symbolic. They had been on the second day of a long-planned vacation when word came that his mother had died. It was too late to attend the funeral, so they stayed on. "The mountains and the beaches have been a restorative," he wrote. "Still, nothing has seemed quite right."

In September, after the *Esquire* article appeared, a friend from my college days wrote to report on his mother's move into a tower for the elderly in Augusta, Georgia, where he lived. "It seems to be going very well," Jerry Chambers wrote. "She's making friends and doing things. I am encouraged, after brooding about it all of July and August."

This was a clear pattern. My friends' parents were reaching the age of jeopardy, and so must mine. Jeff's mother suffered from Alzheimer's, and her death, though a shock, was no surprise. Aside from the fact that he simply couldn't get home to Philadelphia in time, Jeff remained in Europe, he said, partly because when he was a boy, his mother always used to call him in for dinner just as he was starting to have fun. He said, "There I was, just starting this long trip, and she was calling me in for dinner. But this time I had to stay out."

A paralyzing stroke had placed Jerry's father in a nursing home, leaving his mother alone on a remote farm in rural western North Carolina. Twenty years earlier his grandfather had suffered the same fate, but things were different then. "He was paralyzed for four years, and lived at home the whole time," Jerry wrote in another letter.

His wife—my grandmother—was ten years younger, and a bachelor uncle came home from his wanderings to help, lifting him and moving him and things. He never even had a bed-sore. He died at home. The whole family was there when he died, including me, my [twin] brother and my sister. I was seventeen. It was nice.

Today my father is paralyzed by a stroke. He is in a nursing home. There is no practical alternative. But I feel tremendous nostalgia for the way it was, and am convinced that, as deaths go, my grandfather's was a good one: in his own bed, surrounded by wife, children and grandchildren, a host of ministering angels.

My friend said that in placing his mother in housing for the elderly, he felt himself "part of the first generation, in my family, at least, to abandon elderly parents. This is a gnawing guilt that will not be rationalized away."

My parents, meanwhile, pressed on in all their

fragile glory. Barbara and I planned a Christmas visit.

She wasn't always able to accompany me owing to her job, but she and my parents were fond of one another, and she looked forward to seeing them when she could. She worked till noon on Christmas day and we caught a plane at La Guardia that connected in Dallas, where we sat on the floor of an all-but-deserted terminal, daubed caviar on toast, and drank a split of warm champagne in celebration. We were in Guadalajara by nightfall. Mom and Dad were waiting. They seemed bedraggled, but I made allowances, for they must have worked hard over Christmas dinner and it was late; surely they were hungry. I looked forward to sitting down with them. My anticipation rose as we drove in through the gate and carried our luggage to their door.

A tall screen that masked the entrance to our guest room was covered with cheerful Christmas cards, but the table opposite was bare. Mom said, "Are you kids hungry? Let's see, I think we've got some cheese and crackers somewhere." She went to the refrigerator, opened it, and peered inside.

After a moment, she brought a platter to the table.

Hungry and out of sorts, I suggested they open the presents we had brought. There were quite a few, partly to assuage my guilt at not seeing them more often and partly because they had asked us to bring things they couldn't get in Mexico. We had wrapped it all, from Mom's bathrobe and slippers and the radio she needed when she couldn't sleep at night and Dad's new khakis and shirts down to the envelopes of instant grits and bars of Neutrogena soap. "Why don't we wait till breakfast?" Mom suggested.

"No, let's do it now." I wanted some part of Christmas day, some part of the excitement.

They opened package after package with weary expressions of delight. At last Dad rose, yawned and stretched, and said, "What do you say, Mammy? I think it's time for bed."

Mom said, "I thought we'd take you shopping later in the week. We have some things picked out that you might like as presents, but we weren't sure. You'd better see them first." She took her glasses off and wiped them. "We'll see you kids in

35

the morning. Sleep tight." She followed Dad out of the room.

I since have rationalized the disappointment that I felt. They didn't eat late anymore, not ever. If they had, they wouldn't have slept. Cooking would have been exhausting. They had had their Christmas dinner earlier, at a neighbor's. They had assumed we would eat on the plane. Of course it made sense to get us something they were sure we wanted. But I was new to disappointments from my parents.

I was up the next morning making coffee when I heard their cat meowing at the kitchen door. She was savage and delicate, black with yellow eyes. I let her in and she rubbed against my legs and purred for food. I found some in the refrigerator and spooned it into her dish. Dad bowled into the kitchen a minute or two later, yawning and scratching under his old robe. He opened the refrigerator, looked inside, eyed the cat's dish, and looked at me. Sudden fury transformed his sleepiness. He leaned at me accusingly and said, "Did you feed the cat? Don't feed the cat." He stalked off toward their bedroom with his rolling gait.

I was stunned. His reaction seemed unreasonable, and I still was feeling last night's disappointment. "Some people would have said good morning," I complained to his stiff, retreating back. Then I heard Barbara giggling in our bedroom, which was near the kitchen.

"What's so funny?" I demanded.

"You stole his chore," she said.

"So?"

She sat up on one elbow and looked at me, amused. "He needs it. It's what he does in the morning. You interfered." She plopped back down into the nest of covers.

She was telling me I'd taken away a portion of his usefulness, and she was right. I saw that it would have been intolerable for him to give up the management of their accounts. And I thought later that there was more to his reaction. The chore, each chore, was like an anchor, providing a sense of security and continuity. If one day was like the next in its details, then nothing was changing. Time was standing still and they could go on forever.

We went out the next day and chose our gifts, which I no longer remember. A few days later,

Barbara and I rented a car and drove to Puerto Vallarta, where we checked into the Camino Real Hotel. Behind the hotel, workers squatted in a ravine and smoked marijuana as they bundled fireworks for New Year's Eve. The fireworks exploded at midnight over the beach in front of the hotel and reflected in the curls of the Pacific. A mariachi band played "Auld Lang Syne." I want to remember a full moon, but maybe I'm remembering the lights strung in the palm trees around the hotel terrace. There was an old American woman there, alone, whom we invited to our table. When I danced with her, she told me that the secret to making money in the stock market was not to be greedy. We returned to Chapala two days into the new year, and then to New York.

1986

My parents remained in love with their new life. The peculiar and annoying were for them exotic. They tried to have a telephone installed, and were told that with their six-month *turista* permits, it would be impossible. The telephone company wanted a longer commitment before it would string a new line down their street to serve them. No deposit they could pay was high enough. Finally they hired a lawyer, who told them to buy telephone stock and promised to have a phone installed for them in his wife's name. "It all sounds like something out of *Alice in Wonderland*," Dad wrote.

Their permits came up for renewal. The preferred, though illegal, method was simply to pay

Commontal of   John Taylor

—you never knew who, somebody who paid somebody who paid somebody else—and you could sit back with your papers for another six months. Legally, they had to make a trip to the border in the car. A neighbor who had nothing to do drove them to Brownsville, where they got some things out of storage and Dad had his skin cancers removed. After that they decided to apply for *visitante rentista* status, which would let them stay in the country for two years without traveling to the border or paying the *mordida*. The same lawyer filed their application. Dad wrote from his conviction about the world's many conspiracies. "He assured us we were now part Mexican," he reported. "As a matter of record, it took me less time, trouble, and money to get my U.S. citizen certificate in Detroit than it did to get a two-year residence permit in Mexico!"

A conniving preacher and his wife moved in with the old landlady and tried to ingratiate themselves to win her power of attorney, but she kicked them out. Then she fell among the rosebushes and was carried away bleeding. Soon her nephew came to look over the property.

My parents renewed their membership in

Mexico's social security system for the third year. This was such a good deal that the Mexicans no longer permitted new buy-in members. It was like buying into Medicaid benefits for about a hundred dollars. For the first time, they began to use the system. Mom went to the Chapala clinic for a checkup. She received a battery of tests and a supply of her blood pressure medication. "This plus the lab plus the tests, all free," she wrote enthusiastically. "All very professional, too. Lots of young doctors."

The tests apparently showed nothing. Mom said nothing more about them.

"Well, I can truthfully say that I have never seen blood flow so copiously," Dad began one of his letters in March, after they had returned from Brownsville. A blood vessel in his forehead, weakened during the removal of his lesions, had burst when he was bending over to look at a flat tire on the car. He spent the next two months with a bandage on his forehead, and urged me to make contributions to the local chapter of Cruz Rojo, the Red Cross. He wrote to the doctor in Brownsville but never got a reply. "I was in his office thirty minutes, he charged me $150 cash and then turned around and charged Medicare another $350," he complained in a letter. "This is why Medicare is in financial straits. The U.S. health system needs to go to the cleaners to be reamed, steamed, and dry-cleaned."

The year lengthened, and for the most part their letters described their meals and gatherings with friends, the slow turn of their casita and the garden, the bloom of lavender jacaranda and pink-and-white oleander, the books they were reading. *Iacocca* came in for high praise, even from my father, proving the ghost writer's success at making the corporate chief into an iconoclast. Mom was perplexed by Carlos Fuentes's *The Old Gringo*. She read many Latin American authors, including Gabriel Garcia Marquez, Jorge Amado, and Mario Vargas Llosa, and she preferred the dreamlike to the painful, the sweet to the erotic. "I've never been able to figure him out," she complained of Fuentes.

"And so the days drift by," Dad wrote.

He was the old gringo, in my mind. Fuentes's old gringo was Ambrose Bierce, another American who had gone to Mexico to die. But the old gringo in my story wasn't dying, at least not immediately. I pushed my concern for him, for both of them, into a seldom-used closet of my brain. It was always there, but I could let it gather dust.

I started work on my first book that spring. I had been getting more and better magazine assignments, and the book grew out of a story I'd done for the *New York Times Magazine* about freshwater bass fishing, the loopiest professional sport I'd ever seen. I began traveling to tournaments all around the country. My mother could not have been more pleased, or worried. "Please check the weather conditions before you go out on any of the lakes," she wrote. "Do this for your frail old mother who listens to the radio at night and hears all kinds of horror stories." She enclosed a clipping about two fishermen drowned during a Texas tournament when tornadoes hit the lake they were fishing.

Her clippings. She rained them on us. Her letters arrived plump with information from afar, scissored from second- and thirdhand newspapers and magazines. Sometimes the clippings had to do with friends, people they had met through us or knew by our descriptions: writers, reporters, politicians. Sometimes they just struck her as something we'd find interesting. No more clippings, I would beg. I realize now how much I miss those snippets of interest and concern.

I didn't notice the quirks that started appearing in her letters. Now, as I reread them, I see the wrong month, or the wrong year, at the top of the page. Once, she recounted their meal with a friend in Jocotepec, then wrote, "Seems to me I have told you all this [she hadn't]. If so, skip it." During the weeks when they were waiting for their telephone, she included the number in at least half a dozen letters.

1987

In the spring of 1987 Mom announced that she was coming to New York. She and Dad had planned to come the previous fall, but they put it off. Now it was just her. Dad, as usual, took the more comfortable course and stayed in Chapala, claiming he had to look after the cat. I drove to Newark Airport to meet her on a night in May.

All the passengers emerged and I still waited. Then a wheelchair appeared, pushed by a gate attendant. Mom looked lost, but she broke into a smile when she saw me. She pointed for the attendant. "There's my son."

When I reached her, she lifted her watery blue eyes to me and said, "Well, here's your frail old mom."

She started to rise from the chair and the man said, "Let me take you to the baggage claim." The wheelchair made me feel conspicuous. When we reached the baggage carousels, he spoke into a walkie-talkie, then released Mom from the chair.

She held my arm as we waited for her luggage, and leaned heavily against me, apparently exhausted. It was almost midnight, and she had had a long day since leaving Chapala early that morning. I noticed a large bandage covering the back of her right hand; the deep purple edge of a bruise appeared at its edges. "What happened to your hand?" I asked.

"Oh, that." She gazed in wonder at the bandage. "I don't know. I fell. In Dallas. It's just this awful airport. I was changing planes, just going along, and I fell. My legs just went out from under me. The airline people were very nice. They insisted on putting this on it and making me ride around in a wheelchair. I don't think I really need it." She tugged at a corner of the bandage.

I talked enthusiastically about my plans for her as I drove into Manhattan. I wanted her to enjoy the city's theaters, museums, and restaurants. She had written that she didn't want to do much, "just see you and a couple of good movies." But Mom loved theater and music; she had covered the arts in Fort Myers for the *News-Press,* and I was looking forward to sharing what New York had to offer. She had visited the city when she was young, but those trips apparently had not gone well. She had written about sweating through a Labor Day weekend in a too-heavy winter suit and limping through another with new shoes so painful she could barely leave her room. I wanted this time to be different. My book, *Bass Wars,* was finished and I had time to spend with her.

But Mom, who had turned seventy-eight the month before, no longer cared about sampling the wonders of New York. True to her word, she hadn't come for that. Something subtle and basic was at work, a kind of maternal homing instinct. She hauled herself up the steep stairs to our third-floor Greenwich Village duplex, and that was all she wanted. It was as if she needed to place me in my life, almost like seeing me tucked in so she could rest easy in her nights, or in the longest night that she knew was coming.

I urged her out. I'd had to sell one set of

Broadway tickets on the street outside the theater when they'd canceled the previous fall's trip.

"Just let her be," said Barbara.

"But I told her we'd be going to the theater," I complained. "You'd think she'd want to."

"You're her son. She just wants to be close to you. That's all."

We did catch one show. It was a Saturday matinee at a downtown theater of *Rosencrantz and Guildenstern Are Dead*, a play not long on rousing moments. Barbara's mother came in from Queens, and we planned on an early dinner afterward in Chinatown. As we took our seats, Mom complained of being hungry. She wanted chocolate. I bought her a candy bar. She ate it, and fell asleep during the second act. She woke up, and wasn't hungry anymore. Chinatown was out of the question when the play was over. Beyond the hard sidewalks, the crush of people, the cacophony of traffic, Mom was too tenuous to sit while we ate. She might fall asleep again. I felt like a new parent, unsure how to handle her fragility. We went home and ordered in.

On Sunday afternoon, Barbara and I took her to Washington Square Park, near our apartment.

The nearby subway stop connecting with all boroughs makes it one of the crossroads of the city. The day was mild, and some early season sunbathers were sprawled on the patchy grass. Children scampered in the playgrounds. Mothers pushed strollers past marijuana dealers, their dreadlocks stuffed under wool caps, murmuring "Ses, ses." Students lolled around the dry central fountain, where a man with a boa constrictor draped around his neck rode in circles on a unicycle. Young boys leaped on their bicycles from asphalt hills near chess tables thronged with players and kibitzers. Ten feet from the park bench where we sat, a nine-year-old Hispanic boy scrabbled in the dirt as he made a play fortress out of shards of brick.

We knew the boy. He was a circumstantial orphan, the circumstances being a long-gone father and a mother whose main purpose in life was selling her daily dose of methadone to get a drink. Barbara had met him when she was doing a story and fallen for his slippery mercury quickness, which was geared to survival. We were trying to help him and his family, and for a brief time his story intersected with my parents'. As we watched, he brought a whole brick down on his creation and smashed it while he made the sounds of an explosion. "Got 'im," he said with satisfaction, then started to rebuild.

We talked idly, watching it all. It was the only way I could think of to give Mom a piece of New York, to let it pass by in front of her. I wondered what she would have made of the tableau as a reporter. She had an eye for the unusual and a bohemian's tolerance, if not for the drug dealers, certainly for the unicycle-riding snake man. She would have walked right up to him and started interviewing. I remembered her taking notes in a round hand and later typing with her sleeves pushed up, red hair falling over one eye. She typed fast and punctuated each line with a slap of the carriage return until she finished, then she ripped off the paper and leaned back to survey her work. I followed her in life. I never tried to live up to my father. She sat in the park in the sun and basked in the twilight of her maternity until the sun drew low and she gathered her sweater together in the front and we walked slowly home.

She had planned to stay a week. I couldn't see it. I couldn't see what she was getting from her

proximity to our harried lives. We couldn't entertain her, because she didn't want to go out. We
didn't want to leave her by herself. We had talked
about the things we had to talk about. And I was
frightened of her vulnerability, which I could see
at every glance. I wanted not to be responsible for
her. I wanted to get her out of there.

Mom still had keen antennae. We were eating
breakfast the next morning when she looked up
and said, "I think a week's too long. Don't you?"

I changed her ticket and woke up early Tues-
day morning to drive her to the airport. I stum-
bled into her room to wake her and found her up
and dressed, sitting in a sleepy fog on the edge of
her bed. She was dull and listless in the car. At the
airport, guilt would not let me say goodbye. I
persuaded the gate attendants to let me put her on
the plane. Then I remembered she would need
money for tips when she changed planes, so I
changed a bill and talked myself back on the
plane, pressed the money on her as she gazed up,
always, under any circumstances, glad to see me. I
wanted to wrap her up and hug her and protect
her, but I also wanted to be free again, and when I
left the plane I felt both craven and relieved.

We learn from both life and fiction that redemption comes from love, from giving, and yet sometimes the realization comes so perilously late. I loved my mother. But I drove back to Manhattan that morning wondering if I had given her anything at all, and what would save me.

Mom returned safely to Chapala. Her letters revealed little of what I had seen in her. She had enjoyed her visit. The Reebok walking shoes we'd given her were perfect for Chapala's cobbled streets. Beyond that, it was hard to tell she had been in New York at all. Her letters reported news of friends and relatives, the weather, doings in the garden, and trips into Chapala for meals, the post office, and market. She sent clippings. She commented on books.

Of course, I thought from my comfortable distance. My fears were overblown.

Barbara and I had made love and were drinking a second round of Bloody Marys when the phone rang on the last weekend in June. It was my father, and his voice was tremulous.

"It's your mother," he said. "I'm worried about her."

"What's wrong?" I asked, sipping my drink and glancing at the television. Wimbledon was into its second weekend and the matches were starting to get interesting.

"She doesn't know what day it is."

A chill crawled up my spine, but I hurried to rationalize it away. I knew Dad was sneaky about demanding my attention. He was always suggesting that I visit, and was not above hinting at some crisis that demanded it. With Mom recently back from New York and Father's Day just past, it was hard not to suspect he felt neglected. I had gotten deft at resisting his alarums.

"Well, Dad," I said, "that's because they're all the same."

"What's the same?"

"The days. She can't tell the difference because the days are all the same. You get up, go to town, get the paper, have breakfast at La Viuda, go shopping, get the mail, go home. Sunday's the only day that's different. I wouldn't know what day it is either."

"Maybe so, Nick," he said after a pause. "But I wish you'd come down here and take a look at her."

"I'm going to try to come down for your birthday in October, Dad," I said. "I'll try. No promises. Is she there? Let me talk to her." I told him not to worry, assured him she'd be fine, and when she came on the line she said what I needed to hear.

"I don't know what your father's so upset about," she said. "He just likes to worry."

"He says you don't know what day it is. I told him it was because they were all the same."

"That's right. Who cares what day it is, anyway? What's the difference?" she said gaily.

When I hung up the phone, I rolled my eyes at Barbara and went back to the tennis match. But the pattern was now clear, and while I might pretend that things with my parents were the same, they were not and would never be.

I called Dad the next week to ask how she was doing. Better, he said. Good, I said. I told him it was nothing, she just was getting old.

"If what Clarita is going through is part of the aging process, so be it," he wrote later. "I had noticed little things before, such as a little forget-fulness, not as interested in food, etc. But last Friday there was such a sudden change. She would sit at the table and fall asleep, she became vague, just not with it." He anticipated a new regime in which he had to do more cooking and planning for meals. "One naturally thinks of living some-where where they provide one meal a day. They did that at Waynesville Towers. We took one look at what was offered and that was enough. Perhaps we are too picky! I think we can get along on my cooking, supplemented by [our local restau-rants]."

I took some pleasure in picturing my father working harder to take care of her. She was his responsibility, after all. And it was on his insis-tence that they continued to live in Mexico. That was the issue over which we went to war.

Mom's health, both from what I'd seen in New York and what Dad had told me, seemed to dictate their return to the United States. I pre-ferred Florida and Fort Myers. They had a life-time's worth of ties there, it was an easy flight from New York, and the Presbyterian Apart-ments, where they had lived from 1976 through

1982, was within walking distance of everything they needed, even doctors' offices. Dad resisted the idea. The building may have been convenient, but he didn't want to return to the avuncular fascism of geriatric management in an elderly highrise. They had lived in a one-bedroom apartment on a high floor with a view but no pets, not even a bird feeder. Dad had had to put away his tools. He set out birdseed on the windowsills, and the guano police came calling. The management had mandatory fire drills, as if its tenants were in elementary school.

"There is no place in the U.S. where we would be as well off as we are here, certainly not Florida," Dad harrumphed in a letter.

I arrived for his birthday in October determined to settle the issue.

The garden was much changed, Dad said as we were driving from the airport. The old landlady was gone. Her nephew had put her in a nursing home in Houston, and she did not seem likely to live out the year. The garden was certain to be put up for sale. The quality of tenants had gone down. Dad's brow furrowed around the shallow white craters on his forehead as he recounted these indignities.

Mom leaned up from the back seat. "He thinks one of them is after me," she said.

Dad bent around as best he could and looked in her general direction. "What's that, Mammy?" he said.

Mom said, "Never mind."

"One of those characters has his eye on your mother." Dad turned to me again. "I told him off about it, too."

I looked at Mom in the rearview mirror. She was rolling her eyes.

The garden compound had added a satellite dish. It tilted incongruously among the flowers, next to a hibiscus hedge. A man with a gray beard lolled, paunchy and shirtless, in a lawn chair, facing the sun. Dad glared in his direction.

We sat down at the dining table and I dug through my bag for the things I'd brought. Mom craved Nestlé's white chocolate bars, and with them were the foil envelopes of instant grits she and Dad demanded for their Sunday breakfasts, and packages of salad dressing mix. Dad had developed a nostalgia for things English, so I had brought a P. G. Wodehouse collection and William Manchester's biography of Winston Churchill for his birthday, along with a few pieces of Judaica, which was another new interest. It had emerged with my marriage to Barbara and our recounting of Passovers and other celebrations with her Jewish family. Dad had gone out of his way to discover Jewish ancestors in his English past and to declare Judaism the only ethical religion. I was looking for the bottles of vitamin capsules they had ordered from the American Association of Retired Persons when Dad rose abruptly from the table and walked to the front porch. A skinny man in red shorts and a T-shirt was teetering by on the main walk through the garden. Dad stood there like a bird dog on point. "Hello, John," the man called. Dad didn't answer.

"That's the one your father thinks is eyeing me," Mom said. "I told him he doesn't know what he's talking about."

Dad came back scowling. "That s.o.b.," he said. "It's indecent the way he walks around here in those shorts. The rest of the time he's upstairs sucking on a bottle. He drinks whiskey like he thinks it's tea. I like to keep an eye on these rascals, make sure they're not up to something."

"Is it me, or is he getting worse in his old age?" I asked Mom. She was sitting with her hand pressed against the side of her face.

"Oh, brother," she said. "Did I write you about the hearing aid?" She told me Dad had submitted to a visit from a salesman who had fitted him for a hearing aid. But when the man returned, Dad threw him out. He claimed the man was trying to cheat him, and besides, he didn't need a hearing aid. "He says he hears just fine," Mom said. "He doesn't hear a thing."

"What's that, Mammy?" Dad said.

She cupped her hands into a megaphone and said loudly, "You don't hear a thing."

He snorted his disapproval. "I do too," he said.

Mom pressed her right hand to her face again. This was an old ailment, and it was getting worse. Nothing seemed to help the stabbing sensations of the facial neuralgia called tic douloureux, or "painful twitch." It hurt Mom sometimes to talk and eat, and cold aggravated the pain. The fall mornings and evenings were cool in Chapala. Now she rose from the table and fished among the contents of a drawer. She brought out a heating pad, which she plugged in and held against her face.

For the next several days I joined their slow parade around Chapala as I tried to persuade them to return. Mom held my arm as we walked along the rough sidewalks and cobbled streets. Dad walked ahead, into the wind. Mom swayed at each steep curb, like an acrobat undecided about leaving the platform for the tightrope.

"Maybe you should think about a cane," I said one day as she struggled across a broken slab of sidewalk.

"A cane?" Her tone suggested that I needed observation. "I don't need a cane."

Dad measured his breathing when he walked. He timed it to his rolling gait, inhaling and exhaling as deliberately as a scuba diver as he walked the half-block from Chapala's newsstand to La Viuda, the restaurant where he and Mom ate breakfast. I had surveyed with him up and down steep mountainsides in North Carolina when he was in his sixties, but now he paused if he had to walk beyond a block.

"You really do need to come back," I said. "What am I supposed to do if you have some kind of an emergency?"

"I don't care, Nick," Dad insisted. "We just can't live there the way we live here."

In the end he agreed to let me inquire about some retirement communities they'd seen advertised. They proved high-toned and expensive. "All very enticing," Dad wrote, "but all cost more than twice our income." Then the refrain: "There is no place in the U.S. for the elderly who have small incomes and little money."

Bass Wars was published at the end of 1987. I dedicated it to "Clare and John Taylor, my parents and the first writers I knew." They could not have been happier. I was working on a second book. *Sins of the Father* was the story of a turncoat mobster and the family to which he was both a savior and a curse. Mom and Dad greeted this project with cautious approval. They worried secretly that I'd be gunned down in the street. I hardly had time to be worried about them amid the round of book parties, interviews with the ex-mobster and his family halfway across the country, and trips I had to make for other stories. Dad still insisted that they stay in Mexico, and I didn't have the time or patience to try to change his mind.

I called more often. Sunday mornings were the restless times. I'd be in bed with Barbara, reading the newspaper and drinking coffee, mind half on what I read and half on the duty ahead until, reluctantly, my hand would creep toward the phone and I would dial Chapala. I asked the same questions every time, the same questions casual friends ask each other when they're passing on the street, questions that crave answers that will let them keep on walking. "How's it going? How's Mom? Is everything okay?"

"Oh, we're rocking along," Dad would say.

One day he answered with indignation in his voice. "Well, your mother left me downtown this morning. I went into the market and when I came out she was missing. The man at the cab stand said she drove away. I had to take a cab home." He paused, as if he couldn't believe what he was about to say. "She just forgot me and went home."

I couldn't help but laugh at the image of it, Dad all puffed up with certainty, finding he'd been left behind. Mom came on the phone and said, "He was all steamed up when he got home. I said, 'Oh, where were you?'"

1988

Mom's letters began more often to mirror her condition. She frequently dropped dates. Sometimes there were other lapses. But just as frequently the letters were lucid and perceptive. She wanted to know in February 1988 who we liked in the Democratic primaries and whether Bush or Dole would prevail among the Republicans. "Who can lead us out of the woods?" she wondered. She wrote with charm about the change of seasons: "I look out one window and see red, red poinsettias (Christmas and winter) and another to see jacarandas (lavender and spring)."

Dad grew more demanding. By the spring, I began to suspect him of wanting me to take her off his hands, to bring her back to the States

while he stayed there. It was as if the extra attention she required and the extra household duties
he now bore were cheating him of his full measure
of retirement. He also ranted jealously about the
"time, effort, and money" we were spending on
the little boy we were trying to help raise.

By June he was in high dudgeon. "It is time
you gave some thoughts to your aging parents," he
wrote.

I had hoped you would have been down here
before this and we could have discussed the situation. You know how ancient I am, and with a
heart condition; anything can happen at any
time. If anything did happen to me, you would
have to see that your mother was situated without delay, where all her meals were provided,
and where someone would be sure to see that
she got out of bed at a reasonable hour every
day. There are days when it is hard to get her
going particularly if the weather is cool.

The other side of this, is that if I suddenly
found myself alone I would probably go back to
England. I have no desire to live anywhere in the
U.S., least of all in Florida. The U.S. is a less

civilized country than it was forty years ago, and I do not think it is going to get better any time soon. In England my health needs would be taken care of. I would be out of the clutches of the A.M.A.

Dylan Thomas would have tipped his hat to Dad, for in his old age he was raving at the close of day. Not altogether rationally, I thought. He hadn't been back to England since he left, in 1923.

"Oh, yes," he added, trying to rub more salt into my conscience. "If I should check out I want you to take my Bible, the gift of the Governors of Christ's Hospital to me when I left school, and *read* it!"

I wrote back, just as angry as he was, at his polemics, his hysterical demands for my attention, and his ridiculous faith that I could change what he would not.

Every time I have suggested possibilities you have been reluctant to cooperate. A visit to Chapala won't resolve these issues any more than they were resolved last October when I was there because you will only entertain one point of view—yours. If you were more accessible as you were in Waynesville or Ft. Myers, I could see you more often but you're not. I've asked you for information about your assets so I can help you preserve them, not for me but for you, and at the same time try to find a program of assistance, but you have never been willing to tell me anything. I don't want to beat a dead horse, but I still think mom would be most happy in Florida among friends and in a warm climate, but at her expense you have refused to consider it even after I said I'd help pay the rent at the Presbyterian Apartments. You say you won't go back there, that medicine costs too much and so on, but I think one reason for mom's lassitude is the absence around her of people she knows. Moving to another area of the country, with which none of us is familiar, would not improve her situation. Nor can I imagine that either of you would be happy in the New York area. We're not going to be here forever, and one of the places we have in mind is Florida. Meanwhile, I have offered what assistance I can afford to hire the help you need in

Chapala, but you always find some reason that won't work.

He answered,

I do not feel I am to blame for all the dissension you accuse me of. Mamacita and I are in complete agreement that we would rather live closer to you; we are also in agreement that there is nowhere that we would be better off than we are here. We can live on our income here, and we have a good climate. Living in the U.S. we would have Medicare, of course. But Medicare does not mean anything; unless you also have supplemental insurance the doctors won't even look at you. With our income we cannot begin to buy supplemental insurance. For $1/3$ the cost of supplemental insurance in the U.S., we can pay into the Mexican social security health system and have *complete* coverage: doctors, hospitals, ambulance and medicines. I do not know where you get the idea that I am forcing your mother to live here against her will. Nothing could be further from the truth. We both agree that there is nowhere in the U.S. where we could live as well as we do here.

It was difficult to argue with him about the U.S. health care system, which demanded either money or impoverishment. Dad, as usual, had the solution. "The answer, of course, is that you buy a house down here. You would then have a place where you could really get away from it all, with no interruptions, built-in house sitters who pay rent, no heating or cooling problems. You can get a good place here for $50,000 or less."

I read this and felt the burden of his expectations. A house in Mexico wasn't in my plans, or in my budget. I had seen sacrifices made on my behalf and I was grateful, but my gratitude wasn't all-consuming. I wanted to do what I could for my parents, what they would let me do, but I, not they, would have to calculate the cost. I was in the grip of the "sad, strange irony" E. M. Forster describes in *Where Angels Fear to Tread* as Gino lifts his child by Lilia and kisses him. It is the tie that binds parents to children but not children to parents: "If it did, we could answer their love not with gratitude but with equal love, life would lose much of its pathos and much of its squalor, and we might be wonderfully happy." Get away from it all? My second book was now well along, and I had just signed a contract with a major magazine. Barbara and I continued to be part-time parents to the Hispanic boy, now ten; it was exciting, fun, and gratifying, a way of coping with the panorama of need New York presents at every turn. More, there was a sense of possibility with him, a simulation of the parental tie. The last thing I wanted was to get away from it all. And if I had, it would not have been to Chapala, with its dwindling lake and swarms of tourists.

That summer, a new owner took over the garden. Both my parents had extensive dental work, Mom hoping to alleviate the pain in her face; their income failed to cover the expense, and I began sending monthly checks. Toward the end of the year, they talked of moving to Brownsville, Texas. "We could walk across the International Bridge to Matamoros for the Mexican social security for our medicine," Mom wrote. "I know it gets terribly hot and I'm not sure the air conditioning would be good for my facial neuralgia. Anyway, we can discuss it at length when we see you."

A story took me to the Pacific coast of Mexico that December, and I stopped to see them on the way. They no longer trusted themselves to drive to Guadalajara, and one of their neighbors met me at the airport. "Your mother's just not the same Clare we remember," the man said as we swayed along the road to Chapala in his old green Chrysler. He told me how they'd met. He and his wife, snowbirds from Minnesota, had been wandering the streets of Chapala looking for a place to stay. Mom had seen them from the window of the restaurant where she and Dad were eating, decided they looked lost, and waved them inside. "They were the first people we met here," the man said. "They made us feel at home, and we've been friends ever since."

Mom was nodding in the living room when I arrived. Dad was bending over a crossword puzzle at the dining room table. They looked up together, briefly frozen. Then they rose and we converged in hugs and greetings.

I stayed only a few days. I felt as if I was visiting an old house where someone has stayed too long, past the covering of furniture and gathering of dust. We went to La Viuda for breakfast the first morning. They no longer had to order; the waiter knew what they wanted and brought it.

We were walking back through the garden when one of their neighbors emerged to walk her tiny dog. Once they'd been friendly, but now Dad turned on her. "If that goddamned dog comes near me, I'll kick it over the roof," he threatened, his face dark. Mom pulled at him, and he turned and with his rolling walk disappeared into the house. Mom spent the afternoon in her patch of sunlight, holding her heating pad against her face. When the light was gone, she opened her eyes and saw me watching her. "I'll tell you, Nick," she said, "old age is not for sissies."

We all were sitting at the table the next morning when the new owner lumbered across the garden to my parents' door. "Here comes El Gordo [Fatty]," Dad said. The man knocked and entered without waiting, came across the porch and into the living room. He was a big man, size 46 at least, all wrong, too big and too soft and too pink among the leathery brown Mexicans, too full of bustle and insistence to wait until mañana. He had come to raise the rent.

Apology radiated from his unlined face. He was making improvements; he gestured to the stacks of plastic pipe that lay alongside freshly dug trenches, which would improve drainage in the garden. He had to cover expenses. Running a machine shop in Chicago had been nothing like this.

We listened. The man left. Dad looked trapped and embarrassed. I felt a rush of sympathy for him, even as I saw the opportunity to bring them home. All he wanted was to meet his basic needs, health among them, and to have some money in his pocket. The ingredients of dignity were all he asked.

Dad looked out at the garden and his beloved birdbath. He looked back at me and frowned and shook his head. "I don't like it, Nick," he said. "But it looks like we don't have any choice. We'll go back and apply at the Presbyterian Apartments."

"When will you go?" I asked. "I'll meet you there."

"I don't know," he blustered. "We can't leave right away."

I suspected him of foot-dragging, but I had forgotten that Mom couldn't easily leave Mexico without the car. Regulations were designed to prevent North American tourists from undermining the Mexican economy by selling their cars to Mexicans. She would have to put it under bond at the airport, which they didn't want to do, or apply for special permission papers. That's what they chose to do, and settled down to wait.

I left to meet Barbara in Mexico City. Before we went on to the coast, I called them. It was obvious that Mom didn't remember that I'd been there.

1989

The phone rang on a Wednesday late in January. The line, when I picked up the phone, had the familiar hiss of a call from Chapala, and I waited for Dad to tell me Mom had her papers and they would be going to Fort Myers. Instead, it was one of their neighbors. When a neighbor of your elderly parents calls from far away, you will not receive good news. The woman told me that Dad had collapsed that morning at breakfast and was in a hospital in Guadalajara.

Mom was in bed when I arrived in Chapala. She was dozing sitting up, pillows plumped around her. "Oh, Nick," she said when I shook her awake, as if I'd just walked over from next door. "Your father's not here. I don't know where he is."

"He's in the hospital, Mom."

"The hospital? Oh, that's right. Well, tell him hello for me, will you? I think I'll stay right here."

It was Saturday by then. The two intervening days had been filled, for me, with phone calls and assessments and arrangements and rearrangements, the logistical overload of family crisis. During that time, Mom apparently had been oblivious. With Dad not around to get her up, she stayed in bed. The neighbors had been bringing her meals. She seemed untouched by what had happened, as paradoxically fragile and yet buoyant as a light bulb bobbing in a raging sea. Beside her, the small black cat stretched, yawned, and rolled onto its back. I guessed the neighbors had been feeding the cat, too.

It was too late to go into Guadalajara, so I unpacked, showered and changed, and made myself a drink. I felt alone, and didn't want to be, but there was nobody else who could decide what needed to be done. Dad's heart had started to beat too slowly and too weakly to sustain him. The digitalis no longer gave it enough of a kick. It beat so slowly and weakly on Wednesday morning while he was waiting for his eggs and bacon at La Viuda that the blood reached his brain only in a trickle. The brain had too little oxygen to function, and he collapsed as the waiter, Lupe, was arriving with a pot of coffee. By falling to the floor (startling the restaurant cat, Zapata), he placed his heart on a level with his head and made the heart's job easier. One of my parents' friends, a nurse, was sitting at a nearby table, and she made it easier still by raising his feet, in effect pouring blood toward his brain. All that had saved him. To go on living any kind of life, he would need a pacemaker.

I tried to figure out what he would want, what made sense. I could take them back to the United States, but he and Mom together would be too much to handle. I could take him to Guadalajara's public hospital to be screened for an operation, to which he was theoretically entitled as a benefit of his Mexican social security. He would like that; he would think he was getting his money's worth. But the screening could take weeks or months, and approval wasn't guaranteed. It was just as likely that he'd be forced to limp along on digitalis till he died. Somehow I thought that Dad's theoretical fondness for the system would not stand this practical a test. The other option was to pay for the operation where he was.

Night fell and the lights blinked on in the garden's other houses and apartments. A knock came at the door. It was the woman from Minnesota whose husband had met me at the airport. She was carrying a pot of soup. She went straight into the kitchen and, over my protests that she'd been kind enough already, prepared a tray and took it in to Mom. "Poor thing," she said when she came out. "We all feel a lot better now that you're here. Maybe it will perk her up a little."

Mom was awake later when I went in to clear her plate. She had her radio earplug in and was fiddling with the dial, trying to pick up Larry King. She slept fitfully at night. Listening to the late-night talk show was her favorite pastime. Larry King was her American reality, just as Dad's was the political news he couldn't tolerate and the misfortunes of his favorite baseball team, the Atlanta Braves.

"Who's he talking to tonight?" I asked.

She took the earplug out and patted the edge

of the bed for me to sit. "It's not that interesting," she said. "Tell me, when is your father coming home?"

"I don't know. A few days."

"Will he be all right?" she asked.

"I think so."

"I hope so," she said. She paused, then smiled at me with a touch of her old lucidity. "But it has been calm around here for a change."

I drove into Guadalajara in the old Plymouth the next morning, after making Mom promise to get up and wash her hair. Hopital del Carmen was in the western section of the city, in the sector called Hidalgo, on a quiet tree-lined street behind a shopping center. It was a 1950s-style building, placed lengthwise and uninterestingly along the street. I asked for Señor John Taylor and was directed to Room 216.

Dad was lying there looking at the ceiling, fidgeting, obviously bored. "Hi, Dad," I said. He looked up and broke into a big, wide grin. He peered at his watch to show he'd been expecting me, struggled to a sitting position, and swung his legs, spindly under his hospital gown, over the side of the bed.

"I'm glad you're here, Nick," he said as he felt for the floor with his feet. "Let's get out of here."

"Dad!"

He looked and caught me laughing. "What's so funny?"

"It's not quite like that. The doctor says you need a pacemaker."

"Well, good, I'll get a pacemaker. Let's go."

I explained that the cardiologist, a man I'd met only on the phone, was due for a meeting. So was a woman who sold a brand of pacemaker. We had to talk with them and decide what to do.

"You tell me," he said. "Just get me the hell out of here."

Dr. Francisco Javier Robles Torres walked in sometime later. Javier Robles was tall, pleasant, and young, somewhere in his thirties, I thought. He had trained in cardiology at the University of Texas. The pacemaker woman arrived, dressed in a power suit. We spoke in English. Dad followed the conversation carefully, looking at each face in turn. When they left fifteen minutes later, the pacemaker woman had a substantial check and the operation was scheduled for the following afternoon.

"What did they say?" Dad wanted to know.

"Tomorrow afternoon. You'll be home by Wednesday or Thursday."

He looked glum, but he didn't argue. He settled back into the bed with a big sigh. I dug in the bag I carried for a sheaf of crossword puzzles I'd been saving for him. When I left him later, he was busily at work.

I returned the next morning with a change of clothes. A steady stream of neighbors had been busy in Chapala; Mom was well looked after and I was relieved to be able to focus on Dad in the hospital. It seemed to be expected that I would sleep in his room. There was a couch in the room that the doctor had indicated with a shrug.

A ghoulishness overtook me as the hour of the operation neared. I felt I had to be in the operating room. It was something I wanted to see, and I didn't want to miss the opportunity. The doctor looked at me strangely, but he agreed and showed me to the scrub room, where I put on a green operating suit and mask and tied sterile bags over my shoes. The operating room was large, with green tile walls and a faded red tile floor. In an adjoining room, the doctors were choosing their operating music, and when Dad was wheeled into the room a radio was playing a jumpy version of "Walk Right In, Sit Right Down."

Dad was pale. His face was taut with apprehension as a nurse positioned him on the operating table. "We'll have something to talk about after this, won't we?" I said, trying to relax him with a bluff performance.

His expression rebuked me. "You will," he replied.

I watched as the doctor cut a pocket in the flesh over his right pectoral muscle. I watched my father's blood well from the wound. The pacemaker was a shiny steel disk, flat on one end, the size of a large pocket watch. The doctor found a vein, and all eyes turned to a black-and-white monitor as he fished a wire through the vein toward my father's heart. The wire seemed alive, a dark spirillum writing against the gray glow of the screen. On another monitor, Dad's heartbeat fluctuated wildly, barely disturbing the tracking line and then sending it bucking and plunging at sharp angles. At last the barb in the wire's end found a purchase in his heart. The battery in the pacemaker started sending its metronomic signals. The monitor line stabilized in steady blips. I watched life reenter my father's face. A ruddy pink replaced the dead gray pallor. It was like watching a flower bloom. It was amazing. I felt that by being there, I'd somehow helped invent him, rosy-cheeked and new, and I felt an overwhelming tenderness for him I'd never felt before.

Moments later, the steely lozenge tucked away under fresh sutures and stinging his heart seventy times a minute, Dad was wheeled from the operating room.

I spent two nights in the hospital. Late at night, when he was asleep, I sat under a fifty-watt bulb at a small table in the lobby, drinking pallid coffee from a machine and working through the copy-edits flagged on the manuscript of my new book. This is a painstaking process, one that requires concentration, but no one ever bothered me as I worked. I hardly heard a footfall. Sometimes I would walk to the door and look out into the night, and find myself meeting the eye of the night guard who patrolled with a carbine slung behind one shoulder. By the third day, Dad was ready to go home. I put the bill on my American Express card and we walked into a bright afternoon that was warm in the sunshine.

Dad was stiff and sore where the stitches bound him, but he still was so transformed that it was easy to forget that only days before his heart had been about to gutter out. As we neared Chapala he said, "You know, I think I'm a little hungry. I haven't had a decent meal in days. What about some lunch?"

"What about Mom?" I asked.

He looked at his watch. "She's probably eaten already," he decided.

"Where do you want to go?"

"What about La Viuda?"

So he wanted to return to the scene of the crime. I drove past the bullring and their street and into town, made the right turn where the road heads west along the lake to Jocotepec, and parked. A dry smell of tinder and parched earth filled the air as we walked along the street. The restaurant was empty in the middle of the afternoon. Dad looked around, disappointed. He wanted some fanfare. We sat against the wall, away from the draft from the ceiling fans. He ordered a big meal and wolfed it down; I couldn't believe his appetite. He was about to order a piece of cherry pie when he hesitated, looked distressed, and said, "You wait here, Nick. I'll be right back." He rose and hurried off in the direction of the bathroom.

Damn, I thought, cursing him for ignorance and gluttony and myself for being stupid. I got up and followed him.

He was straightening up from the sink when I walked in. He looked chastened and a little pale. "I'm all right. I just ate too much," he said. He was determined to put on a good face, and added, "I think I'd better skip the cherry pie."

Mom had roused herself for his return. She was sitting in her chair, wrapped in sweaters, heating pad against her face. She rose slowly as we entered the house. Dad walked straight to her. "Hello, Mammy," he said.

She offered him a kiss. He pecked her on the lips and she placed a hand against his cheek. "How are you?"

"Sore as hell." He unbuttoned his shirt and pulled down his undershirt to show her the bandage.

"Look at that," she said. "It's been awfully quiet around here."

"Has it? That's good." He yawned suddenly. "I think I'm ready for a nap. What about you, Mammy?"

"Aren't you hungry?" she asked.

He looked guilty for about half a second. "No. We just ate. At La Viuda. I had beef Stroganoff. It didn't agree with me."

"You did?" She looked vaguely disappointed. "Where was I?"

"You mean you haven't eaten yet? Nick thought you'd probably eaten." He looked at his watch, yawned again, and yawed off toward their bedroom.

"Thanks a lot, Dad," I called after him.

"Don't worry, Nick," she said. "I've had more food than you can shake a stick at. People have been bringing me food all week. Good, too. Better than your father's cooking. I'll just have a little snack." She rummaged in a drawer, found one of her white chocolate bars, and followed him into the bedroom.

While they slept, I started to pack for the trip home. I thought I could leave safely. Dad functioned well enough to look after himself and Mom, and if I stayed he'd expect to be treated like an invalid. Besides, there was nothing to do but wait for the papers that would let them leave Mexico without the car.

When I took my suitcase from the closet, my eye fell on a heavy cardboard box stuck away in a back corner. It was stiff and sturdy, made with handholds in the ends for lifting and as fondly familiar as such a mundane item as a cardboard box can be. It bore the marks of Barber's Apple Orchard, where my mother had worked around the time that I was born. It had moved with them from place to place ever since I could remember. I lifted the box from the closet, removed the lid, and looked inside.

Among the papers and folders the word "Argonaut" stood out, embossed on what looked like a leather cover. I drew it out and opened my mother's high school annual, Iron Mountain High

School, Class of 1927. I found her picture moments later amid a predominance of jug-eared Swedes. She hadn't started wearing glasses yet. Her hair was cut in a flapper bob. The caption over her five lines of activities read, "She is small, but so is a stick of dynamite."

Soon my hands were covered with the dust of old papers: postcards and letters, business cards, photographs, clippings, story proposals. As I looked through them, I saw my mother as an ingenue, full of life and promise, then as a career girl, then a young wife, then a working mother. Her first job out of college, probably the only one she could find in those early Depression years, was as the sole reporter for the *Rising Sun,* a Muslim weekly in Chicago. She had worked at the Chicago World's Fair. She had worked in Detroit for the American Automobile Dealers' Association and for J. Walter Thompson, the advertising agency. Apparently, from the exchange of letters that I read, she could have gone somewhere in advertising if she had accepted a transfer to New York. She had written well-crafted and ultimately fruitless queries to magazines; I knew something about that.

I sat on the floor, the dust of her memories thick on my hands. She had a broader life than I had known. Still, I thought, what if? What if she had been born in a time more receptive to her talents? What if she had been more ambitious? What if—most intriguing—she had gotten to New York and not had shoes too tight, had left her hotel room and walked around the city and fallen for its rude charm and energy and spark? Of course, it is only happenstance that produces each of us. Coincidence upon coincidence leads to every birth. Then we try to defy coincidence for the brief span of our lives, until we are taken by coincidence. There is no what if. There is only was and is and will be. I could have no regrets about my mother's life.

That night after supper, instead of retiring to read in bed or tune in to Larry King, she asked to see my manuscript. I was pleased. I brought it out, almost five hundred pages, and she sat in the living room next to the cold fireplace and started reading. I expected her to get a flavor of the story, be suitably impressed, and go to bed. She kept reading. She read and read. I sat opposite her, trying also to read but glancing at her furtively.

She held the manuscript in her lap and turned the pages one by one against her chest. When there were too many and they started to collapse, she placed them face down on the coffee table and went right back to reading. I drank one glass of brandy, then another. The house grew chilly. Dad came in from the bedroom and stood at the edge of the light. "When are you coming to bed, Mammy?" he demanded. "I'm reading Nicky's manuscript," she said. He stood a moment longer, grunted, and retreated. Mom read on. Or seemed to. I couldn't tell whether she was just looking at the pages or actually reading.

"You don't have to read the whole thing, you know," I said.

"Oh, no," she said. "I want to."

Eleven came, and midnight. I was getting dizzy on Pedro Domecq. The pile of pages on her lap grew steadily thinner. Finally, at about one o'clock, she turned over the last page. She sat there for a moment. I waited. She looked up, blinking.

"What time is it, anyway?" she asked.

"It's late, Mom. Almost one," I said.

"Goodness." She took her glasses off and rubbed her eyes.

"Did you like it? What did you think?" My voice sounded loud to me. I wanted her to have, if only for a moment, the authority I'd seen that afternoon when I was looking through her papers. With it, I wanted her to give me back her praise.

"Oh, yes. It was quite a story. I didn't like him, though." She was talking about the mobster at the center of the book. She shivered to show her distaste. "That poor wife. And those kids." She heaved herself forward to get up, flopped back in the chair, and tried again. I went to help her.

I walked her to their bedroom door. "Thanks for reading it," I said, and kissed her on the cheek.

She looked at me fondly through exhausted eyes. "You're a good kid," she said.

I couldn't seem to get my parents moved. My friend from college, Jerry Chambers, couldn't keep his mother in one place. We had continued trading stories about our parents since he'd moved her into the high-rise for the elderly near his Augusta, Georgia, home; it was a form of reassurance and, sometimes, a way of laughing through the tears. His paralyzed, stroke-ridden father breathed on like clockwork in a nursing home. His mother, sharp-tongued and independent, had passed her third year in the high-rise. Those three years apparently had enlarged her love of independence.

Bertha Chambers had left Augusta for a few days the previous October. She told Jerry she was going to the mountains to enjoy the fall colors. The farm where she had lived most of her life was nestled in a high cove. I had been there once. A creek ran behind the house and splashed down to a lake in pools and rills. The red and white oaks, the sweet gum and maple and honey locust trees, would have been brilliant in autumn. The leaves were not through falling before Jerry received her letter saying she wasn't going back to the high-rise in Augusta.

"And furthermore, she said she didn't want to pay the next month's rent," he told me later. "She wanted to know could I pack up her things and get them out of there real fast."

Jerry agonized at this, as he had when he'd placed her in the high-rise. His mother was eighty-one, and the farm was so remote that a rifle shot wouldn't have reached the nearest house. But she was strong. She also was insistent, and he did as she asked. I told him he was lucky.

My parents were inertia-bound. Mom's papers came through, the permission she needed to leave Mexico without the car. They had four months, but Dad's doctor advised him against traveling right away. Beyond the delay was the problem of where they would live. The Presbyterian Apartments had a six- to eight-month waiting list, in the event they were accepted. It wasn't clear they would be; the building, like many, wanted only people who could function on their own. Without Dad, Mom would need regular care. And Dad, after the initial euphoria of his survival, dropped ever stronger hints that he wanted to be free of his responsibility for her.

"I can take care of one person, but not two. I don't exactly feel like jumping over streetcars," he told me in one of his calls. They had been more frequent, and fretful, since his operation.

I tried to think of my father's life. He never had been looked after, really. His early years were painful, I knew from an account he'd written at my urging. His mother had been sick, an alcoholic whose liver failed when he was five. With her death, his father was widowed for the second time. His prosperity had rotted, along with his oranges and dates, in the London dock strike of 1911, and he went to Zanzibar. When he returned, he lived in rooms in men's clubs. My father, mending slowly from the operation on his hip, was unwanted goods. He lived with an uncle, then with various retainers and friends. After one move, he recounted, "That first night I remember waking up in tears and Lady Lindsey coming into my room and trying to console me. This was something new. To have someone show affection was a new experience and I was not quite sure."

Later he was packed away to public school, Christ's Hospital in Horsham, where he received the Bible he had suggested that I read. "All through my school years, where everyone else had a home to go to when holidays came around, I had none," he wrote. "At the end of every term I experienced an agony of uncertainty of where I was going." Once he slept on a cot in his father's room at the Primrose Club in Jermyn Street in London, another time on a sailboat moored in the

Crouch River, where he cooked breakfast for his father each morning and stayed alone on the boat each night while his father rowed to shore to eat supper at a yacht club. Little wonder that he wrote, "I felt fortunate to be invited to stay at the home of a school friend."

In February 1923 his father gave him his gold pocket watch and its heavy gold chain and put him aboard an ocean liner leaving Southampton. My father waved from the deck. He was sixteen. He reached Canada, took a train to Detroit, moved in with his half-sister Irene, and went to work. His father died that May.

To rest, to be cared for a little bit at last, was what he wanted now. At this late juncture of his life he was transferring his responsibilities to me. But I wasn't about to let him off the hook so easily.

"I'm not convinced that the two of you can't live reasonably independently," I wrote.

I think Mom will perk up when she gets back to Fort Myers, and I think that even if you don't feel 'like jumping over streetcars' you can still help do the basic chores required of an

99

independent couple. I was aghast when you asked me about Shady Rest. Dad, Shady Rest is a nursing home, and neither you nor Mom is ready for a nursing home quite yet. You said you could take care of one person but not two, but if you think the best solution for both of you is for her to be in a nursing home or some other kind of home without you, I strongly disagree. Of course, I'm sure that's not what you had in mind at all.

The point is [I lectured], it's not time to give up the business of living. As long as Mom can get interested in things again, and I think she will in Fort Myers, she'll be able to participate in a reasonable style of living that will require your help. You have to remember that you two are a team, have been for almost forty-seven years now, and you must continue that way.

Okay, there's no way to know what is available without my going to Ft. Myers. So Barbara and I will make a trip there in the next couple of weeks. By the time you're ready to travel we should have some idea about the options.

. . .

Barbara and I drove from her sister's home in Fort Lauderdale and checked into a hotel on Lover's Key, the island just below Fort Myers Beach. "The Beach," as the locals call it, is an island, too —Estero Island—but this lovely name, derived from the Indian tribe that once inhabited the area, is hardly used today.

A stiff March wind had hollowed out the sky and driven the tourists inside. The wind raised whitecaps on Big Carlos Pass, where, I'd always heard when I was growing up, the founder of the oddball Koreshan religion was lying in a glass-topped coffin. The story was not entirely apocryphal; the tomb of Cyrus Teed, who called himself Koresh, was swept off Fort Myers Beach by a hurricane in 1921 and never found. Stranger was the Koreshan belief that our world is the inside surface of a hollow globe and the universe we know is a swirl of gases in the center. God would not have created an infinite universe—so went the Koreshan line of thought—because human beings cannot understand infinity and God would not have created something we cannot understand. There were never very many Koreshans. There might have been more, but they were celibate.

Winter-season traffic had backed up at the one stoplight on Fort Myers Beach. We waited forty-five minutes to get off the island. The road into Fort Myers passed shopping centers where truck farms and gladiolus fields had been. The desire of northerners for warmth had converted sandy muckland and scrubby stands of pine into subdivisions full of houses on quarter-acre lots. It had erected hotels and apartments at the water's edge. Somewhere in all of this, I hoped, was a place for my parents.

But where? Their bohemian life had left them with meager resources. Groucho Marx refused to belong to any club that would accept him. I didn't think my parents, unless they could still live independently, would live in any place they could afford. Barbara and I had made a lot of phone calls, and we didn't expect to find a retirement home for seven hundred and eighteen dollars a month that didn't make us shudder. The seven eighteen was the total of their Social Security checks. It would cover their rent at the Presbyterian Apartments. There wouldn't be much left, but I could help them a little. They also had about fifty thousand dollars in their various accounts, thanks in part to a bequest from one of Mom's sisters. That would let them live nicely for a while, but it would go quickly. They could outlive it. When it was gone and they had no money at all, they would have no choice but Medicaid—medical welfare—and someplace sad with stale odors.

That puzzled me as infinity confounded the Koreshans. It seemed to me the spiral of comfort should lead up, not down. People who slept early on coarse muslin should lie on linen at the end if they've a little money set aside. But the luxocracy of health care forced them to give up the dignity of a small nest egg, or juggle to save it against catastrophe. A lawyer I knew specialized in "estate preservation." He told me to make sure my parents didn't have an estate. I had written to my father, "You will have to appear to have no assets. If you have any, the government will make sure you spend them."

We drove through Fort Myers's downtown. It was painted and hung in old Florida colors to attract people from the malls, but it slept on. A few blocks east, we turned into the parking lot of a tall building whose name made it sound like a resort. I guess that was the idea. Calusa Harbor was supposed to be one of the best of the ACLFs —adult congregate living facilities—on a list the state had sent us.

An efficient young woman showed us around. The place was bright and clean, with a medical staff and a dining room. It offered three levels of care: independent living, assisted living, and a nursing home. The independent living package came with one meal a day and weekly cleaning and linen service. Assisted living included services such as help with dressing and reminders to take medications. I could see Mom and Dad living there. They would be safe and well looked after. Services would increase with their needs.

"How much?" we asked. The least expensive one-bedroom apartment cost almost twice their monthly income.

We drove a little farther east and turned into a residential neighborhood. Following directions Barbara had scribbled in a notebook, we found our way to a place that looked like a fifties-style motel. There was a central building that once must have been a private home, flanked by two separate residential wings.

A woman met us at the door of the main

building, and took us into a lounge full of men and women dully watching television. Outside a big picture window, a walk led through a coarse lawn to a dock that poked into the windswept Caloosahatchee.

Our host offered to show us the room the facility could offer my parents. "They like this," she said, "they" apparently referring to the generic elderly, as she led us along an open walkway. "It makes them feel like they're getting outside."

The room was the size of a motel room, with old wooden furniture, unremarkable framed prints on the walls, a bathroom in green tile, printed draperies. Shrubbery, or the eaves, blocked light from the windows. There was a refrigerator, but no kitchen; three meals a day were served in the dining room, which looked across the lawn to the river. The extra meals made the place more expensive than Calusa Harbor. We backed away, bobbing up and down with false assurances that we'd be sure to call.

"What are we going to do?" I asked Barbara when we were in the car.

She kicked off her sandals and propped her bare feet on the dashboard. Her hair was black then, before the tints and highlights that changed her to the redhead she said she was always meant to be. "Keep looking," she said. That was one of the reasons I loved her: her indefatigability.

But by the end of the afternoon I was ready to give up. We had crossed off the list places that were too far out of town or masquerading boarding homes. Every other place was too expensive or too shabby, or both. We had had no better luck with apartments. We had looked at buildings with sun-faded cars parked out front and loud music playing behind every hollow door. We looked at a converted hotel in the somnolent downtown. We interrupted a card game in a garden apartment that was advertised for sale, where the owners told us everything was so convenient, as long as you could drive. We finally returned to the Presbyterian Apartments to find the waiting list just as long and the application requirement intact. "No, we don't make exceptions," said the man behind the desk. "Even if they lived here before, they might not still be qualified."

We were near the river then, a little west of downtown, so we decided to probe one of the nearby side streets. It was an area of small offices, struggling motels, and old homes, the kind starry-eyed young couples dust off into bed-and-break-fasts, anchored by apartment buildings at the river's edge and a shopping center that contained a Woolworth's and a Kash-N-Karry supermarket. The street ended at the river. On one side was a new apartment building where the rental agent quoted prices that were far too high. The building across the street was squat by comparison. Its sign announced it as the Riverside Club.

"Let's go over there," Barbara said.

"Oh God, what's the use?" I complained. "Let's go back to the hotel and get a drink."

"Come on," she said. "It's right there."

I sighed and huffed my way to the door of the Riverside Club, where we met a man who told us to call one of the numbers on the directory at the door. After several minutes, during which we took stock of the swimming pool and landscaping, a white-haired woman emerged. Her name was Bess Jones. She cocked her head when I asked if she had anything to show us. "Oh, honey, I sure have," she said.

"Do I know your parents?" she asked as we waited for the elevator. I gave the thumbnail history and she exclaimed, "Why sure I do!" Bess said she remembered my mother's *News-Press* by-line and knew several of her friends. She explained, volubly, that the seven-story Riverside Club had been Fort Myers's tallest building when it was built, in 1965. "They called it a sky-scraper," she said, chuckling. The people who bought its condominium apartments were mostly old-timers who predated the area's rapid growth; they remembered Hurricane Donna and the rickety swing bridge to Fort Myers Beach. I decided that for my parents, it would be like finding Briga-doon.

We looked at several apartments, but the one that fit them and the one we could afford was a one-bedroom on the seventh floor, facing the river. It was owned by the estate of a woman who had died. Her homely velveteen furniture came with the place. We agreed to buy it anyway, for forty thousand dollars.

"Dad, it's perfect," I said when I called them with the news. "No fire drills. You can walk to restaurants, so you don't have to cook if you don't want to. No rent to pay, so you can get someone in to clean. You can manage it. I know you can. And Mom will love it."

"I don't know, Nick. You know I don't feel like jumping over streetcars. But I guess it's worth a try."

I confirmed the deal and, from New York, arranged the necessary money transfers.

Feeling there was no more time to waste, we worked quickly to ready the apartment. We especially wanted Mom to feel at home there. Before we left Fort Myers, we hired a decorating service to repaint, to rip out the dingy olive carpet and replace it with Mom's favorite shade of green. We ordered matching sun-reflective window shades, a new dishwasher, and a rattan living room set in a splashy tropical floral. I thought it would remind her of a sofa we had once that she had liked. We called a secondhand store to pick up most of the old furniture. I arranged phone and electric service and set up a savings account to receive their funds.

I left it to Dad to arrange their end of the move. I felt a little guilty about this, but it seemed straightforward enough. He could contact the movers, show them what to pack, and keep out of the way. I didn't want to return to Chapala. I didn't think I'd have the patience for it, and there really was no need. They would fly to Fort Myers and we would meet them.

They set a date in the middle of April. Barbara and I returned to add the finishing touches. We scurried through the Edison Mall buying kitchen utensils, linens, lamps, a vacuum cleaner, a remote control TV, and a phone with a volume control. We took dining chairs to be recovered. We unwrapped and washed their blue-and-white Haviland wedding china and stacked it in the cabinets. We stocked the kitchen with staples and their favorite foods. It was as if we could make the apartment beautiful and welcoming enough to overcome my parents' frailties and negate my father's doubts, as if by giving it life and charm and brightness we could renew theirs.

Bess looked at all the work we were doing. "Are your parents all right?" she asked.

Just fine, I told her.

"Oh my, I wish you were my children," she said.

I spent the last day before they came in a do-it-yourself shop, framing some of my father's prints and watercolors.

Framing pictures suited me. It is intricate work, requiring attention but not much thought, and the mind wanders. You start by placing lengths of frame molding into two vises set at right angles to each other and fitting their mitered ends together, then tapping in brads to fix them. Then you go on to the next corner, and the next. My parents were coming home. Bedraggled birds on their last migration. Whatever happened next would be easier. It had to be. They would like their new apartment. I thought of it as theirs, although the deed was in my name and Barbara's. Odd to say, but I was encouraged that its previous owner had died there, or approached her death. That translated it somehow into an end point, a terminus. The woman had lived alone, struggled with her illness, endured her infirmities there, in that apartment, and that meant my parents could do the same. Dad would have to do his share in taking care of Mom. But they could manage. Mom's friends would help her to renew the spark she'd lost. So would the pictures I was framing, laying glass into one of the completed frames now and wiping the back clean.

Suddenly I felt the gaze of the other people in the shop and realized I had laughed out loud. I had been thinking of my father in a retirement home, unleashing his temper around blue-haired ladies and doddery men, something about the food, maybe, or the television. The woman in Chapala with the dog had told me, "We're going to miss your mother, she's just so sweet, but your father . . ." She shook her head and twisted her mouth around an imaginary lemon, and I had nodded in complicity. That was enough reason to keep Mom and Dad independent as long as they could manage it; it was just good manners.

I laid a piece of art into the frame behind the glass, stood it up, and studied it. It was a watercolor he had done in Mexico, adobe buildings and blue sky. I added the backing, fixed it with staples, sealed it with Elmer's Glue and paper, screwed a pair of eyes into the frame, and twisted on a length of wire. Then I started on another frame.

The apartment was beautiful when we left to meet them the next day, April 15, two days before

Mom's eightieth birthday. It was spotless, with all the pictures hung and all the conveniences in place. We backed out of the door trying not to disturb the freshly vacuumed carpet, congratulating ourselves with every step. At the airport, their plane arrived almost as we did, and we didn't have to wait at all. The old gringo limped off the plane on full alert, casting around fiercely. He looked relieved when he saw us. Mom produced a fleeting smile and said, "Look who's here. Your frail old parents."

Bess and her sister managed to be around the door of the apartment building when we returned. Bess made a point of knowing what was going on at the Riverside Club. She fussed over Mom and Dad and told them how much they were going to love their apartment. "These kids of yours did so much work," she said.

"I hope they didn't do too much," Mom said.

"We won't be here that long," Dad said.

"That's right," Mom added. "We're going back to Mexico as soon as possible. We have to get our Social Security straightened out, and then we're going back."

"You are?" Bess drew out "are" into two or

three syllables. Her squarish face wrinkled in perplexity.

I didn't know if this was wishful thinking or delusion, but I turned to Bess and whispered, "I don't really think so." Turning back to my parents, I said, "You'll have to be here for a little while, I guess, so why don't we go on up?"

The elevator droned its slow way to the seventh floor and we clambered out with their luggage. I gave each of them a set of keys to the apartment, Mom's with a coiled plastic bracelet so she could wear them on her wrist and wouldn't lose them. Dad opened the door and they went in and looked around and nodded and didn't say anything. Mom went into the bedroom and sat down on the bed, got up, came into the living room, and sat down on the rattan sofa with the floral print. Dad peered at the pictures, one by one. He went to the window and looked out at the river.

Finally Barbara said, "Do you like it, Clare?"

Mom said, "It's very nice, for something somebody has set up for you."

We took them to dinner that night at a restaurant that had been their favorite when they lived at the Presbyterian Apartments. Dad liked the prime rib with horseradish sauce. Mom ordered shrimp. They were tired from the trip, and Mom seemed as if she were trying to pick her way through cobwebs. Barbara and I were antsy. When we got to the coffee, I said, "You just got here. Why are you talking about going back to Mexico?"

"Oh, my desk is just a mess," Mom said. "I didn't have time to clear it off."

Dad leaned forward. "What's that, Nick?" he said.

"I wondered why you were going back to Mexico so soon."

He dribbled some coffee from his saucer back into the cup. "Oh. Well, I have a doctor's appointment in two weeks," he said.

My troubles were over. My parents were safely back in the United States, and they weren't going back to Mexico. I knew it, if they didn't. They couldn't afford it, for one thing. I had spent most of their money on the apartment.

Barbara and I returned to New York the next

day. Barbara's mother told her we were leaving too soon, that my parents needed emotional support in addition to a place to live. But we had spent ourselves. Neither of us had the patience for a hand-holding transitional term.

That Monday I spent an hour on the phone talking Dad through opening a checking account at the bank in the nearby shopping center. He had the money from their Mexican accounts, and Mom had surprised me by digging in her purse and producing four hundred dollars that the owner of Chapala's newsstand had given her for the old Plymouth. I explained to a sympathetic woman at the bank that he'd be coming, then told him how to get there and what to say. Barbara, meanwhile, sent Mom a birthday package of clothes by Federal Express.

Six days later, I was aboard a small boat sailing from Bermuda to the Azores. A friend of mine was taking his boat home to England. I love sailing, but the main appeal of the two-week ocean passage was the relief from concern for my parents that the adventure would provide. I assumed they would reorient quickly to Fort Myers.

Mom's first letter had encouraged me, and I sailed with a clear conscience.

"Dear Kids," she wrote.

Someone brought the parcel from New York up to me from downstairs. I am at present enjoying the blue-and-white-striped top. As soon as I locate a dressmaker or someone handy with a needle I'll have the skirt shortened and then I will be able to appear in public. I want to thank you both very much for all the Banana Republic goodies. Very comfortable even with the sun pouring into the dining area window (Does the sun pour?). Whatever, it's bright and hot.

A man called from Social Security to tell us that you had given them our change of address. Thank you, for I've never been able to get them on the phone from here. Why? I don't know. Excuse me while I take time out to get some ice water.

We went to Woolworth's this morning for breakfast. Tomorrow we're going to try the Oasis. We're looking for something to take the place of the Viuda, which was our favorite eating place in Chapala. We've been looking at all

117

the good things available at the Kash-N-Karry, which used to be something else. Neither of us remembers the name. (Thank heavens I'm not the only one who has a lapse of memory.)

The sun is about to go down and there's a nice breeze blowing in the window. We've been enjoying the macaroons from Entenmann's. Is that in New York? A sail boat is speeding downriver. Good view from the dining table. Thanks again for everything. You're good kids and we love you a lot.

She wrote again the following Sunday, commenting on the dining table view of "birds, pelicans, and boats, barges." They still were looking for the perfect breakfast. The letter sounded disjointed but conjured perfectly for me the scene and discussion between them, Dad shaving, then grumping and stomping about: "I'm waiting for Pappy to get dressed so we can go out to breakfast. Where? Captain's Table, perhaps. We're eating right here. Have been out for the paper. Now Pappy's getting breakfast."

She put the letter aside and started again later in the day: "Good breakfast. But the lamb chops we had for dinner tasted like shoe leather or what I imagine shoe leather must taste like. I'm going for a ride with Bess Jones at 6 P.M. Now for a nap. More later."

Bess had turned out to be a godsend, a kind and genuinely concerned person who had looked at all the work Barbara and I had done and translated it into interest in my parents. She saw the work as special; therefore my parents must be special. Mom's longtime friends welcomed her one by one and celebrated with a reunion of the Birthday Girls, friends who for years had feted one another on their birthdays. But Bess, who lived on the floor below and saw them day in and day out, became their closest ally and in that way their monitor.

It was Bess who called after I returned from the Azores in the middle of May to say that they still were living out of their suitcases. She said that Mom had nothing to wear except a pair of baggy shorts. We called to ask Mom about the clothes we'd sent for her birthday. Most of them were still in the box. Mom hadn't been able to cope with having the skirt shortened; she told

Barbara the job was "too tricky." Their shipment of household goods, which included most of their clothes as well as their books, Dad's tools, and Mom's apple box of memories, had not arrived from Chapala. Dad was vague about the succession of movers involved.

"I don't know, Nick," he told me. "Just track it down, will you? I need my hats. It's hot as hell down here."

The movers in Guadalajara told me the shipment had been handed at the border to a Texas company affiliated with United Van Lines. The dispatcher assured me it was on its way. It was the beginning of June, more than six weeks after they had moved, before Dad called to say it had arrived.

I found an opportunity to see them two weeks later, when I could tack on a business trip. I got a list of doctors from the county medical society and phoned for appointments. "Ft. Myers is a lot easier to get to than Chapala, so I'm glad you're there," I said when I wrote to tell my parents I was coming.

I flew to Fort Myers on June 17 and rented a car at the airport. The retiree driving the rental car bus mopped his brow and said it was mighty hot, but it sure did beat Rochester. On the twenty-minute drive into Fort Myers, I played with the buttons of the radio, looking for a station. The scanner hit some country music and I stopped it there. The rawness of it seemed to suit my mood. It was all about sadness and memory and loss and struggle and yearning. Traffic was light, and I made good time. The white-painted Riverside Club gleamed in the sunshine at the river's edge. I parked the rental in the covered space for 701-A. The front door of the building was unlocked, so I went in without ringing and rode the elevator to the seventh floor. The door to their apartment was open.

Dad was sitting on the sofa in his khakis and a tatty undershirt, intent on a crossword puzzle. Mom sat opposite, nodding in a chartreuse recliner that had been the one piece of velveteen worth saving. A magazine was folded in her lap. The windows were open. A breeze off the river sang through the screens like someone blowing across the mouth of a Coke bottle. The packing boxes filled a quarter of the room, standing unopened where the movers had left them.

"Jesus Christ!" I blurted in a flash of irritation. "Didn't you put anything away?"

Dad only heard my voice. He looked up and broke into the smile that always amazed me with its directness and sincerity. He was glad to see me, and the fact that I'd seen him smile as warmly at a waitress arriving with a cup of coffee didn't make me feel less churlish for my outburst. "Hi, Nick," he said, laying the puzzle aside and rising to greet me with a hug. His skin was damp with sweat. Mom's head jerked up. "You're here," she said, and clambered to her feet.

"It's awfully hot in here," I said after a minute. "Why don't you turn the air conditioner on?"

Mom patted her cheek and grimaced. "My neuralgia," she said thickly. "I'd use my heating pad, but I don't know where it is." She gestured toward the boxes.

"We've been waiting for you to get this stuff out of the way," Dad said.

I checked my anger and started to unpack the boxes. The clothing boxes were the hardest, so tall and deep the only way to get the clothes out was to lift them straight overhead, as if I were a weight lifter trying to press a macrame barbell. No wonder Mom and Dad hadn't been able to unpack. For some reason, Mom still had wool suits. Some of them must have been fifty years old, and they weighed a ton. Finally I had their clothes hanging in the closet, their eclectic library arranged on bookshelves, and their kitchenware, linens, and papers put away in drawers, on shelves, and within cabinets. The job had taken hours, and I finished with the sober knowledge that tasks I had taken for granted were beyond them.

I was setting the empty boxes out for collection when I realized something was missing. "Mom, where's that box of yours?" I asked.

"What box?" She looked up from a travel magazine that contained a piece of mine she had read several times already.

"The box of your things. The apple box."

"Isn't it here? I don't know."

"I can't find it. Dad, where's that box with Mom's things in it? It was in the closet in the guestroom in Chapala."

"What things?" he asked. He had found his straw hats and was sitting on the sofa with one in his lap, carefully smoothing the brim.

A black vision began forming in my mind:

Dad had decided that the box wasn't important and told the movers to leave it behind, because to send it would have cost a few more dollars. Or he had just grown impatient and told them to forget it. He'd left things before when he'd decided he couldn't be bothered. The losses had sometimes been painful. He'd abandoned the bookbinding press he used to make his prints when they moved to Mexico the first time because it took up too much room in their old Volkswagen. The press was a beautiful relic, a sculptural tool of wood and steel in which two flat plates were brought together by turning a wheel on a worm gear. When I asked the couple who'd bought my parents' house if they still had it, the woman refused to give it up. She'd been using it to repair books at the elementary school where she taught. Who could argue? He'd also left behind the blocks from which the prints were taken, and they had been discarded, the painstaking work of his hands. I couldn't imagine that Mom's box had simply been forgotten. I'd unpacked some other things— Dad's carving tools and drawing pens and pencils —from the same closet. I described the box and its contents in detail.

"I don't know, Nick. Everything that came is here." He tried the hat on, took it off, and gingerly fingered a dark spot on his forehead. The squamous cells were acting up again.

I retraced my search, irrationally peering behind chairs and into corners. "You couldn't have left it. Tell me you didn't leave it," I finally wailed.

"Oh hell, Nick, you can't keep up with everything. What difference does it make, anyway?" Dad snapped.

"I wanted those things."

"Well, maybe if you'd been around when we were trying to get packed. I can't do everything myself, you know. And your mother wasn't any help."

"I'm sure it will show up," Mom said. "Who's hungry?"

I brooded while we ate at a cafeteria. Paper clips and rubber bands had made it to Fort Myers. They had brought calendar dishtowels from 1984 and 1985 and frying pans shaggy with dried egg. I had found a desiccated chunk of beeswax Dad had used when he was sewing the sails for the boat he'd built thirty years before.

Later, when I called Chapala, the new landlord, the former machine shop owner from Chicago, said there might have been a box. Yes, his wife had wondered that they'd left it, there were photographs and all. But if it was in the house they must not have wanted it, so out it had gone.

I could have slept on the convertible sofa in the living room, but I rejected the thought. The sofa was too depressingly close to the evidence of my mother's confusion and Dad's dependence. There was a Ramada Inn practically next door to the apartment building, and I took a room there. The motel restaurant was right on the water.

"Oh, let's go there," Mom said the next morning when I went to pick them up for breakfast. Woolworth's lunch counter had become their routine breakfast stop, their La Viuda in Fort Myers, but it was closed on Sundays. Mom was gaily dressed in a pair of white pedal-pushers, an India print cotton top, and a loose jacket of azure blue. The outfit was such a contrast to her person that I had to fight against seeing her as sadly girlish, like an actress who denies growing older, but it was just what she'd put on that morning, not an intent to hide her age. Dad was wearing khakis with a sprung stitch that exposed the zipper.

"Why don't you change those?" I suggested.

He looked down. "Oh, hell. Who cares?" he said, and pulled his shirttail out.

I drove them to the restaurant, although it was only a five-minute walk. On a short open stretch along the river, two men were standing with fishing rods angled out over the water. A third lay along the concrete bulkhead, his head propped against a cooler.

We took a table next to the streaked windows that rose from floor to ceiling. The large dining room was full of families dressed for church. There was a buffet, but Mom and Dad ordered from the menu—eggs, toast, and grits. I chose an omelet and we settled down with sections of the paper. Now and then someone from another table would pass us on the way to the buffet at one end of the room. We paused from reading when our food came, then went back to it over refills of our coffee. I had checked the baseball scores and was reaching for the comics when Dad pushed away from the table. "I'll be right back," he said.

He walked with his rolling gait to the buffet. He peered at it for a moment, then ducked and reached into one of the trays and snatched a piece of bacon. He gobbled it. Then he snatched a piece of sausage from the next tray and wrapped it in a napkin. This he brought back to the table and shook out onto his plate. I looked around nervously to see if anyone was watching.

"There," Dad said. "I always like a little bonus." He speared the sausage with a fork and popped it in his mouth.

I looked at Mom. She shook her head.

"What?" Dad said.

I looked at Mom again, and this time we burst out laughing. Dad watched us. After a minute Mom took her glasses off and wiped her eyes. "What were we laughing at?" she said.

"Your husband."

"Oh. He's funny sometimes, isn't he?" She reached out and patted my father on the hand.

"Why, thanks, Mammy," he said. Then he asked her if she was going to eat her remaining piece of toast.

Mom *had* cleared her desk in Mexico; its contents were jumbled in a series of manila folders that I had stuffed into desk drawers in my parents' bedroom in my rush to put everything away. That afternoon, while they slept, I tried to put her papers in some kind of order. I took the folders into the living room and sat at the dining table, where the blue slant of the river and the line of its far shore came through the translucent blinds. Gulls wheeled behind a small boat moving among floats that must have marked crab or lobster traps. I didn't quite understand how reflective blinds could be translucent, but they were, admitting the view and diffused light while hot strips of direct sunlight burned at their edges.

The first folder I opened contained several life insurance policies. One was a cancer policy, one a travel accident policy from AAA, another a policy that paid in case of accidental death or dismemberment. There may have been a fourth. The annual premiums were low, and she'd paid them faithfully, in the case of the cancer policy for almost fifty years. But over the past year, the payments had petered out and stopped. The reminders were filed, unopened. All the policies had lapsed.

It isn't the money, I thought as I closed the folder and went on to the next. The awards were too low to make much difference, and in any case, she wasn't likely to die in a way covered by the policies. It was how forgetfulness had thwarted her intent that wrenched at me. It was like seeing little pieces of her fly away.

The next folders contained old check registers and bank records. I looked through them and returned to the bedroom to see what else I could organize. Dad was sitting up against his pillows as he slept, snoring gently, his legs stretched out in front of him. Mom was curled up under a baby blue afghan, her hands under her cheek.

I arranged half a dozen photo albums on a shelf over her desk. She had set out photographs of me, and me and Barbara, on the desktop in dime-store frames. I found her fat address book stuffed between a sheaf of book reviews and a ten-year-old diary that contained mainly shopping lists. Mom had been a voluminous and steady correspondent who was accustomed to sending a hundred Christmas cards. I opened the book. She had scratched out and added addresses that tracked her friends around the country. I closed the book and put it into her desk drawer, where I saw her writing tablet. She had started a letter on the top page, set it aside, and not returned to it. It hung there, mysterious and incomplete.

She was disintegrating that way, piece by piece, in lost shards of memory and conversation, in neglected matters that were once routine, in letters begun and never finished. She was losing the gravity to hang on to them, and they were spinning out of her orbit into unknown, un-remembered space.

In the refrigerator, where I went to get a beer, I saw some of the "good things" they had found at the Kash-N-Karry: bags of yogurt candy, bars of chocolate, a box of mint candies. The freezer contained cartons of ice milk next to the TV dinners and pot pies I had stocked for them. I closed it and looked around the kitchen. Their dishes were stacked in a sink rack; the dishwasher I had waited all my life to give them was empty and dry.

All the evidence told me they were on the

fragile edge. Dad's health seemed relatively good; their network in Fort Myers provided a system of warning and support; they still could get around. Beyond that, I was traveling on faith.

We walked to breakfast on Monday morning. I wanted to be sure I wasn't kidding myself that they could get to the shopping center and back. It was about a ten-minute walk from the Riverside Club, across a street with light but sometimes dangerously fast traffic. Dad walked ahead, rolling side to side, head down. He angled off to buy a copy of the *News-Press* from a coin box. I followed with Mom at a slower pace; it was early, but already hot. We crossed the street with me acting like a shepherd: Come on, come on. I was relieved when we reached the relative quiet of the shopping center and the shade of its covered walks.

Woolworth's lunch counter was a throwback, with booths and stools in salmon-colored leatherette and Coca-Cola signs with pictures of hamburgers and grilled cheese sandwiches on them on the wall behind the counter. A statuesque waitress with cascading auburn curls greeted Mom and Dad warmly. "Oh my, this must be your son," she said, looking at me in a way that made me wish I were a little more awake. "We've heard so much about you, your writin' and all. Do you want coffee? I know your mom and dad do. Don't y'all?" When we were settled in the booth and the coffee was steaming up in front of us from thick white mugs, her partner, plump and motherly, arrived. Pencil poised over her order pad, she said, "What'll you have, honey? I know what your folks want."

A procession of regulars came and went for the next hour. The waitresses, whose names were Louise and Ann, kept filling our coffee cups. The store's manager came to say hello. The voices of bickering old men rose from the booth inside the window, next to the display of beach chairs. Bess, her sister Rae, and two other women from the Riverside Club entered talking; they, too, were part of this informal breakfast club. It was the focus of my parents' day, and I found it comforting. I had called enough aging programs by now to know that they all placed a priority on activities: games, shopping trips and other outings, concerts, sing-alongs. The Woolworth's breakfast club was an activity. I could keep encouraging them to live independently as long as they had it to look forward to.

Having established that they could get to Woolworth's on their own, I didn't force the point by making them walk home. I got the car and drove them.

The medical appointments I'd made for them began that afternoon. Dad grudgingly agreed to see the cardiologist I'd chosen. He hated doctors —or feared them, I wasn't sure which—but he also desperately wanted to know that his pacemaker was going to keep ticking. The doctor was pleasant, in his thirties. I sat in the examining room with them and explained what I knew about Dad's pacemaker. The doctor pressed a stethoscope against Dad's chest, and Dad jumped and said accusingly, "That's cold." When the doctor was through listening, he shrugged and said, "Seventy beats a minute, like clockwork. It's working fine. I'd like to keep an eye on him from time to time."

"Hear that, Dad? You're still alive," I said.

"Huh? That's good, I guess," he answered,

buttoning his shirt over the outline of the pacemaker. "Let's go get something to eat."

"We can't, Dad," I told him.

"Why not?"

I told him I'd scheduled general checkups for both Mom and him, one after the other, at an office within walking distance of their building. I wanted to know there wasn't more wrong with them than there needed to be. He grumbled and sulked when I told him we'd have to eat late, so I dropped him off at the lunch counter and told him to order a sandwich while I took Mom to her appointment.

Mom went uncomplainingly. The doctor who saw her gave me no serious new worries. He said, "She's got nothing unusual for an eighty-year-old woman. You should watch her diet, though. It seems to me that she's anemic." He said he wanted some blood tests run, and handed me directions to a laboratory.

I thought I could leave Dad for his checkup while I ran to the laboratory with Mom. But when I picked him up he said, "Goddamnit, Nick, I've already been to the doctor once today." I didn't feel like arguing. I called to say that we'd reschedule, dropped Dad at home, and drove Mom to the laboratory. The distances weren't far, but the logistics had been daunting. It was more than they could have handled on their own.

Dad resumed his griping the next morning when I left him at Woolworth's to take Mom to an early neurology appointment. I now took her confusion as a given, but I hoped something could be done to ease the stabbing pains in her right cheek. We came away with a prescription, but no information about additional warning signals. I restocked their refrigerator with low-salt, no-fat dinners whose labels made claims about nutrition, wrote checks to pay their bills, and returned to New York more conscious of their frailty. I only hoped they could, as Dad had started to put it when we talked on the phone, "rock along" a little longer.

"Nick?" It was Bess's voice on the telephone. My name had never had so many syllables.

"Your dad wanted me to call. I'm up here in their apartment. Honey, I'm afraid your mother's had a little stroke. We're waiting for the ambulance right now."

It was early on the morning of July 4, just over two years since Dad had called to say Mom wasn't herself.

"Is he there now?" I asked. "Can he come to the phone?"

"Nick, your mother's had a stroke," he said when he came on the line. He sounded scared.

"Are you all right?"

"What? I don't know. I tried to get her out of bed this morning and she couldn't sit up. She just fell over. Bess is here. We're waiting for the ambulance."

It must have happened while she was asleep. A CAT scan would show the clogging of her carotid arteries—the main arteries leading to the brain. The diminished flow of blood and oxygen was what caused her confusion. Then a clot broke loose from an artery wall and found its way to a vital juncture. Morning came, and when she tried to respond to Dad's rousing, something was shockingly missing. Her left leg and arm had deserted her, jumped ship in the darkness.

Dad spent the day at the hospital, but when I

talked to him that night he could tell me nothing new. He was concerned about Mom, but he couldn't hear well enough, and was probably too frightened, to deal with the information. All he could deal with was his own discomfort. Bess said that while they were waiting for the doctor to arrive—a long wait on the holiday—he had suddenly announced that he was hungry and insisted on going out to breakfast.

Mom's neurologist told me, when I finally got in touch with her, that she had "poor expectations" for Mom's recovery. Given that, the doctor added, "We have to be concerned about your father's ability to care for her alone.

"Did the hospital ask if you wanted her resuscitated?" she asked. "If she goes into arrest."

I thought a moment before answering. My mother had made clear in her living will that she didn't want to live at all costs, didn't want just to go on breathing. "No, don't resuscitate," I said.

There is no preparation for a stroke and the incapacity it causes, certainly not on the part of the victim. In the case of someone my mother's age, the humane thing to hope for is death or a complete recovery. Most of the stages in between are a kind of purgatory. When the emergency had passed and Mom was still alive, but now with a leg that dragged and an arm she couldn't lift, she entered therapy to relearn how to walk. The physical demands on her were greater than they'd been in years.

While Mom struggled in rehabilitation and Dad with the new terrain of loneliness, I encountered an octopus of regulations. Medicare would pay for Mom's hospitalization and treatment as long as she was making progress, that is, recovering some of her mental faculties and her ability to get around. When she stopped making progress, Medicare would no longer pay and she would be discharged. Maybe Dad could care for her, and maybe not; it depended on the extent of her recovery. The apartment was too small for someone to live with them, and anyway I could not afford it. I could put her in a nursing home, but I didn't want to do that if I could help it. Another option was occasional visits from an agency that provided home care for the elderly. The right thing to do eluded me.

At the same time *Sins of the Father* was about to be published, I'd just contracted to turn the story of the mobster and his family into a screenplay, and I was preparing a new book proposal to put before my publisher. These events competed with my parents' needs for my attention. I talked to Mom on the telephone. Her speech was unaffected by the stroke, but she couldn't tell me what to do with her.

Mom regained some use of both her leg and her arm, but she couldn't walk without assistance. She remained "in limbo about whether she wants to go home or to a nursing home," according to a social worker at the hospital. Peggy Williams, part of an eight-member social work staff, was part hand-holder, part guide, and part interpreter. She was my reassuring point of contact with the hospital. The use of social workers in medical institutions of all kinds has become widespread in the past twenty-five years. They help families cope with their anxiety and grief, and with the tangles of regulations governing their options. In that way, they help divert patients to less costly types of care.

Rehabilitation took Mom as far as it could take her, and a discharge date was set. I had not found a better answer, so she went home. I begged

Dad just to try it, to see if he could handle the greater help she now required. The specter of their separation was as frightening as anything that might happen to either of them individually. I didn't think they could function except as a unit.

Mom suffered a second stroke before his ability to care for her had been well tested. The doctor described it as a kind of aftershock. It weakened her left arm further, but she went home without additional rehabilitation because it would have consumed more of the Medicare days she was allotted. The experiment was a disaster.

First came the unsettling report, relayed by Bess, that Mom was living on a diet of sausages and ice cream. "I'll have you know John Taylor is a very good cook," Mom told the friend who looked askance at her nutrition.

She fell, and he couldn't lift her. She called to him for help one day as he was shaving, and he left the water running as he went to her. Water reached the fifth floor before somebody came up to turn it off. The insurance claim was almost four thousand dollars.

I tried a home health care service, which sent a nurse—rehabilitation therapist. It wasn't enough.

The service's coordinator told me, "They need more help and supervision in daily living than they're getting."

By then—it was late August—Dad was calling every day. "Nick, I can't hack it. I just can't hack it," he said despairingly.

Mom's third stroke obviated my decision.

The nursing home was across the river from Fort Myers, in a suburb that was now larger than the city. Barbara and I came straight from the airport and picked up Dad at the apartment. He rode in the front of the car, bracing himself with one hand on the door and the other wedged against the seat. The light through the windshield made him squint. His hair had a reddish tint where he brushed it back from his high forehead, and I thought that he must be putting Mercurochrome on the resurgent skin cancers. He poked his stiff leg out in front of him, and drew the other up. We wound among tract houses, turned onto a busy boulevard, and after a couple of miles found the nursing home on the left.

An ambulance was parked under a portico

that protruded from the center of the low building. Double wooden doors opened onto a long hallway. Dad, inclined as if he were walking uphill, led the way. A group of mostly women in housecoats and bathrobes sat in an open lounge at the end of the hall, clustered around a television set. The nurses' station was opposite. Dad ignored everybody and veered right down a branching hall. Barbara and I followed, nodding courtesies. He reached a door on the right, turned back to us, and said, "She's in here."

Just then a flustered nurse caught up with us and said, "Are you looking for Clare Taylor? She's in therapy."

We retraced our steps to a door off the main hall. We opened it and entered an L-shaped room. Mom was standing between a set of parallel waist-high bars that ran the length of the room. She was canted to her left, struggling to grip the bars, shuffling one step at a time. A large man in a white uniform supported her with ham-sized hands on her waist and encouraged her to keep moving. In a mirror along the back wall I could see that her chin was thrust forward in her old attitude of determination.

When she saw us, she tried to lift her left arm like a broken wing to wave. "Oh, boy," she said to the therapist. "Can I stop now?"

"Let's just go to the end, okay?" he said.

She shuffled to the end of the bars and turned awkwardly to sit in the wheelchair I'd taken there. She turned her face up to offer me a kiss. I saw endurance in her eyes, a kind of patience with suffering, and a mother's full quotient of trust and love, which can never be equaled.

"You looked good up there," I said.

A flicker of some inchoate emotion crossed her face, as if she'd formed an opinion she wasn't ready to express. "It's good to sit down," she said.

We made a procession back to her room. There were two beds; hers was nearest the door. The woman in the other bed was whimpering, and when we entered and I helped Mom up on the bed, the roommate said, "Get the nurse. Please get the nurse."

"She's always calling for the nurse," Mom said.

"Nurse, nurse," the woman called.

"Oh, be quiet," Mom said under her breath.

We sat for an hour. The woman in the next

bed whimpered intermittently and called for the nurse. Just outside the room at the end of the hall, a man in a wheelchair was rolling himself furiously at the emergency exit door, as if it would shrink in fear and open. He would stop just short, back up, and propel himself at the door again, forward and back, forward and back, compulsively. A nurse came into the room and said it was mealtime. We started to say our goodbyes. "Aren't you going to stay for dinner?" Mom asked.

"Not today, Mom," I said. Dad was restless, and the home really wasn't set up for dinner guests.

She pouted, but when the food came she turned her attention there.

The man in the wheelchair was muttering as we passed. He was saying, "This is no place to die, no place to die."

For the next ten days, Barbara and I stayed at a rented beach house on Captiva Island. I spent each morning on a shaded porch fifty yards from the Gulf of Mexico, working on the screenplay. Each afternoon I drove the thirty miles into Fort Myers, picked up Dad, went to the nursing home to visit Mom, took him to lunch, and then, in one small office or another, tried to plan ahead. Barbara stayed behind with a project of her own to work on; she could add nothing to the planning, and as much as my parents liked her, the truth was that at this point, they wanted only me. The people at the nursing home were very sympathetic when they told me they could keep Mom as a Medicare patient only as long as she was making progress in her rehabilitation. Then Medicare no longer would pay. What then? The social worker at the nursing home, whose name was Henry Klein and who, I would learn, played guitar in a reggae band on weekends when he was not counseling the shell-shocked relatives of patients, cocked the heels of his cowboy boots on the edge of his desk, ground a cigarette into an overflowing ashtray, and ignored for a moment the constantly ringing telephone. He told me to apply for Medicaid.

I called for an appointment and a day or two later walked with Dad into the state welfare office to describe my parents' poverty. This humiliating exercise meant going down a list of things they didn't have: car or truck; motorcycle; burial insurance; trust funds; life insurance; burial plots; real estate; business equipment; boat; stocks or bonds. They owned nothing beyond the small checking and savings accounts I had set up with the money from their Mexican accounts. Their only income was their Social Security checks. It was not enough, however, to own nothing at that moment. They had to have owned nothing for three years; that is, any assets they had transferred within the past three years would count as assets, and the value of those assets would have to be spent on their care before they were dirt poor, and then, only then, the health care system of the richest country in the history of the world would provide for their long-term care. I saw my father moving from the apartment into a housing project, and determined to lie. That turned out to be unnecessary, because by adding my name to their accounts more than four years earlier in Mexico, they had in effect transferred their assets then.

Dad looked gaunt and stormy when I took him in to sign his application form. He hadn't had his favorite khakis fixed; the zipper still pooched out, but I had decided I didn't care. He had earned his eccentricities. And he was a good prop when it came to proving poverty. He didn't look like somebody trying to beat the system. He looked as if he needed help.

To travel with Dad around the city was to be a hostage to his appetite. I ate several meals at a restaurant near the nursing home that baked sandwiches in flowerpots. But he was equally a hostage, and I shanghaied him one afternoon to the Sears hearing aid department.

"I don't need a hearing aid," he said as we weaved through the barbecue grills and lawn mowers on our way to the hearing center.

"Dad, we have to spend your money anyway. We might as well spend it on a hearing aid." That was true. I had to submit their bank records for the Medicaid application, and the balance had to be below three thousand dollars.

He sat glumly in the waiting room. I said, "Dad, you're alone now. You've got to know what's going on."

"I can hear what I need to hear," he said.

The certified hearing aid examiner, a tall, older fellow with the solicitous manner of a civic club member in good standing, looked in Dad's ears with an examining tool and asked him some questions. After a while he nodded gravely and leaned forward to look Dad in the eye. "You have profound hearing loss in one ear and about seventy percent loss in the other," he said.

Dad raised his eyebrows in disbelief. He said, "I have?"

The fellow brought out a hearing aid. It was not one of the subtle models that snugs inconspicuously inside the ear, but the kind that fits behind it, hung on like a backpack. He said to me, "The smaller ones won't work with your father's hearing loss. He needs one with more power." Dad looked at it, turned it over, sat uncomfortably as the man placed the plastic case behind his ear and pushed some waxy stuff inside his ear to make a mold. We left with a promise that the hearing aid would be ready in a few days.

Afterward we walked slowly through the mall. The local Corvette club had filled the mall with candy-colored hot rods that Dad surveyed with bland amazement. We went into a bookstore, and after he disappeared for a few moments I found him rearranging copies of my book so they'd be more visible. We sat on a bench near a trickling fountain sprinkled with pennies. I said, "Dad, what would you change if you had it to do over?"

He thought for a long moment, then shook his head.

"Well, would you have worked more on your art, tried to make a living at it, maybe?" I couldn't imagine him not having regrets, even if they were along the lines of Wilfred Brimley playing Kathleen Turner's grandfather in *Peggy Sue Got Married.* When she asked him the same question, he said, "I wish I'd taken better care of my teeth."

Dad shook his head again, decisively this time. "I can't think of anything," he said.

We left the mall and headed for the nursing home.

We arrived to find Mom, jaw clenched, chin prognathous, negotiating the hallway behind a wheeled walker. A therapist trailed her discreetly. "Oh, goody," she said when she saw us. "Get my wheelchair, will you?"

"Don't you want to finish, Mom?" I asked.

"No, I want to lie down."

She had a sling around her neck. I forgot what it was for until she was in the wheelchair and I started to turn her in the direction of her room. Her left arm dangled, and I saw just in time that her fingers were twined among the spokes of the wheel. A turn of the wheel could have broken them. She reached over and picked up her arm with her right hand and dropped it, lifeless, in her lap.

Dad and I helped her into bed. Her roommate stirred and immediately called out, "Nurse, nurse."

Mom said, "Oh, shut up."

The hours in the nursing home seemed endless. Dad sometimes would take a letter he'd received to read to her. But he always exhausted his supply of conversation quickly. Then he would move to a chair beside her bed, work a crossword puzzle if he had one, or just sit, not in any nobility of patience but in suspension, waiting. I exhausted the supply of magazines and *Reader's Digest* condensed books in the nursing home's small library (which was always empty in preference for the television area) looking for something that would interest Mom, but she no longer sustained much interest in anything she read. I would leave the room and return to find her sleeping, glasses lying in an open magazine. I tried to entertain her with news of my work, to which she would listen with attention. I took her a small radio with an earphone so she could listen to Larry King at night. Believing that sometimes kindness and lies, as Graham Greene wrote, are worth a thousand truths, I spoke to her of the time when she would be home again.

Freed from caring for my mother, Dad went swimming. Each afternoon when we returned from the nursing home, he would change into a pair of swimming trunks, take a towel, and head downstairs. He was a sight with his pale, skinny legs and his pacemaker bulging in his chest. He would lower himself gingerly into the pool and swim in place for a few minutes, climb out dripping, and trail water as he returned to the apartment. I couldn't explain this sudden interest—as far as I knew, it was years since he'd gone swimming—but I was encouraged by it. Anything that took him out of the apartment and into the world could be good for us both.

We returned to pick up his hearing aid. The examiner wiggled the earpiece into place and made a few adjustments, and Dad walked out wearing it. Here again I saw the potential for new life and increased independence.

Barbara and I returned to New York. I began a round of interviews and book parties and intense days of collaborative writing on the screenplay. I spoke with Dad almost every night. I always asked him if he'd been to see Mom. After a short time his visits began to grow infrequent. If Bess wasn't going he had to take taxis, and he didn't like to wait for them or spend the money. I, too, was neglecting Mom. Reaching her by phone at the nursing home was almost impossible, and each day was so packed with writing that at the end I wanted nothing but to stop. But eventually I wrote:

> Dad has had a little trouble getting out to see you, Mom, because Bess Jones has been away. I've been encouraging him to take cabs. It's expensive, but he tells me he keeps opening drawers at your apartment and finding wads of Mexican pesos. When I was there we found 320,000 pesos, and he told me that he found another 500,000 pesos last week. It amounted

to about $250 altogether. So he has some found money he can use.

Henry Klein there at [the nursing home] told me Friday you're still doing therapy. This means that you're still making progress in getting that left side working again. I know it's discouraging to have to work so hard when you want to take it easy, but I think it's worthwhile in the long run.

Well, it's Saturday afternoon, pleasantly and unexpectedly warm (Indian summer), and I'm going to try to make a little progress in revising the screenplay. I expect to be off on a new book project before long. So I'll say goodbye now. Barbara and I think of you a lot, and I know you think of us, too. Much love and many warm thoughts from both of us.

A week after we had arrived back in New York, the nursing home called in a frenzy. "Your father told us yesterday he was taking your mother out for the afternoon. She came back at eleven o'clock this morning. If she hadn't, she would have been discharged against medical advice." The woman paused to let me absorb this. "And Medicare would not have paid," she added.

"What did you do?" I asked Dad when I got him on the phone. "Did you lead some kind of jailbreak?"

He chuckled, sounding pleased with himself. "I went to see your mother and she said she wanted to go home," he said.

"So of course you took her home."

"Yes. I called a cab. And then the next morning Bess came upstairs and said the nursing home was frantic and that she wasn't supposed to be gone overnight. Nobody told me."

I asked him if he had been wearing his hearing aid. "That damned thing," he said. "I don't like it. There's too much static. I can hear better without it."

On my next trip to Fort Myers, in November, Dad surprised me with a question. "What's this about cassettes?" he asked.

I explained that there were audio and video cassettes. I said, "Some have music. Some have movies."

"Movies," he said.

We went to Wal-Mart the same day and bought a videotape player. A rack near the check-out line held a selection of inexpensive movies, and we bought a compilation of Laurel and Hardy shorts and *The Snows of Kilimanjaro*, with Gregory Peck. I hooked up the machine and played the Laurel and Hardy tape. Dad watched avidly for a few moments. He said, "That's really something." Then he picked up his paper and folded it to the crossword puzzle.

The next day we were driving past the old Fort Myers airport, now a general aviation field, as a small plane came in over the road for a slow landing. "You know, Nick," Dad said, "I think I'd like to learn to fly."

"Fly?" I cut a glance at him. He was gazing through the windshield, looking quite intrepid, as I remembered him at the helm of his boat, which he had named after my mother, but also quite old. His forehead was ravaged, the hair tinctured, the whites of his eyes a mucous brown. The hearing aid protruded behind his ear like an astronaut's jet pack. I had made him put it on before we left the house that morning. He reached up to adjust it.

"Yes," he said. "I've always thought I would."

"Why didn't you?" I asked.

"I don't know. It was always something."

I wish I could say that at that moment I

turned the car around and found a pilot who would take us up. I thought about his heart, his hearing. But somebody in love with romance would have done it, put Dad in a front seat with redundant controls so he could touch them and feel the plane move and see out over the cowling to a horizon that held whatever he was looking for. Or maybe not. "It takes a long time to learn to fly," I said.

"Does it?" he said. "I think it would be nice, though."

We drove on.

That night I spoke to Barbara on the phone. "He wants to learn to fly," I said.

"Of course," she said.

"What do you mean, 'Of course'? He never in his life said anything about wanting to learn to fly."

"Yes, but Bess said her sons were pilots. Don't you remember? She said they'd flown down to see her in their private planes. This isn't about flying. It's about Bess."

I felt a moment of joy at life's essential silliness when I hung up the phone. Dad had a crush on Bess. I should have seen it coming. I recalled how brilliantly he smiled when she walked into Woolworth's and sat down with us. And she had told me, punctuating the story with indulgent laughter, of how he rushed to claim the front seat each time she offered him and another man from the apartment building a ride to breakfast. I could not be angry with him for what this implied about his feelings for my mother, only happy at the stirrings of life. The old cock still crowed, if feebly, proving the beautiful longevity of our illusions.

Mom had a suitor of her own, in any case. The nurses told us one of the other nursing home residents was taken with her. The man they pointed out occupied a wheelchair and, when I saw him, always wore brown clothes. He had thick glasses and tufts of black hair and followed her around with a wacky, smitten smile. She paid him the courtesies, but that was all.

She languished in the nursing home. Her Medicaid application was approved. Her rehabilitation reached its peak and her therapy wound down to a daily dose of maintenance meant to keep her from declining. With a shuffle of paper and the scratch of a pen, she changed from a convalescent, implying a future, to a permanent resident. Most of the residents gathered before the television set in the lounge opposite the nurses' station, but Mom wasn't drawn to the pacifier, with its game shows and soap operas, the way the others were. She had never watched TV. Her habit would have been to read, but she didn't want to do that either. She preferred to lie in bed.

Toward the end of the year, a bed opened at a nursing home five minutes from the apartment, and Mom was moved. Dad started to visit her regularly again. I, too, settled into a routine, flying to Fort Myers every month or six weeks.

1990

That winter was the inaugural season of the Senior Professional Baseball Association, a Florida
league of major-league retreads. One January day I
took Dad to see the Fort Myers Sun Sox, in second place in the league's Southern Division, play
their first-place rivals, the West Palm Beach Tropics. Terry Park had changed only a little from the
field I remembered as nirvana to a Little Leaguer
and the winter home of the Pittsburgh Pirates
when they won the 1960 World Series from the
Yankees, despite scoring only a dribble of runs
against the Yankees' flood. I bought the best tickets and we settled behind home plate to watch the
game.

The Senior was not a league for pitchers' duels. Amos Otis hit a prodigious home run for the Sun Sox and trotted around the bases in his striking green and yellow uniform. Dad said, "Look at that." But the Tropics' pitcher stiffened while their batters wore down Sox journeyman Steve McCatty, who had won and lost in equal numbers for the Oakland As. The Tropics scored with regularity, raising dust that hung over the plate.

I kept one eye on Dad as we watched the game. I felt the need to be solicitous of him. We were in the shade under the stadium roof, and when he shrugged down inside his jacket I asked if he was warm enough. He shifted on the wooden seat and I asked if he was comfortable. He said he was hungry, and before I went to the concession stand I asked him if he'd be okay.

The visitors won the game. We let the bulk of the crowd go before we got up to leave. "Well, that was fun, Nick," he said. "It would have been better if they won, though."

"Oh, well," I said.

We walked slowly out of the grandstand and in the direction of the car. "What should I do with this?" he asked, holding up the souvenir program.

"Hang on to it," I said. "Maybe someday it'll be a collector's item." It came to me as we made our slow way to the car that I had taken my dad to his first baseball game.

I now slept on the convertible sofa on my visits. Dad went to bed early, and I would flee the apartment in the evenings to play Scrabble with a high school friend and her husband. I returned late, to read or flip channels. Dad often arose in the night to go to the bathroom. He would pause in the hall and stare into the living room, looking like some ghost ship under gossamer sails in the undershirt and shorts he refused to have replaced. I would pretend to be asleep.

We ate breakfast each morning at Woolworth's. Dad's face shone when Bess came in with her coterie. She and her sister sometimes would join us, and we would have to put the paper away, but he didn't mind.

When we arrived at the nursing home around noon, we usually found Mom in the room that served as lounge and dining room. A corridor with offices and patient rooms on each side shot straight through from the entrance lobby to the back, where the lounge opened up and another hall led left, to more patient rooms. The staff would have assembled the patients for lunch before the trays came down from the second-floor kitchen. One of the women wore a bicycle helmet, which kept her from injuring herself when she beat her head on the table. Sometimes Dad and I would sit with Mom while she ate. At first, she would ask us to join her. The home prepared no extra trays, but I tried to accommodate her by eating a bite of something from her plate. Dad would eat her dessert if she let him get away with it. She would ask nervously if we had tipped the waitress when the tables were cleared.

I still would have to take Dad to lunch at one of the seafood restaurants or cafeterias that he preferred. Afterward, I would take him back to the apartment for his nap and return to the nursing home.

Mom would be in her room by then. Her bed was nearest the window, which looked across a parking strip and a grassy ditch to a wing of the hospital on adjoining grounds. There was a bulletin board on the wall. After Valentine's Day it had sprouted cards with hearts and frills, containing messages from schoolchildren. "Mrs. Tailor, I am thinking about you and hope you get well soon," said one. The cards were well-intentioned, but it was difficult not to resent the project's pity and assumption of abandonment, as if no one else cared and hoped and thought, least of all someone who knew the patient well enough to spell her name correctly.

If I was lucky, Mom would be up and sitting in her wheelchair. If not, I would try to get her up and into the chair so I could take her out. This usually meant lowering the bars on the sides of her bed before maneuvering her into the chair. The nursing home attendants kept raising the bars, and this frustrated her. If the bars kept her from falling, they also imprisoned her and forced her, whenever she wanted to go to the bathroom, to fumble with her one good hand for the call button dangling by the headboard. "I don't know why they keep putting these damn things up," she said. When the bars were out of the way, she could swing her legs over the edge of the bed, sit up, and slide till she touched the floor. She was able to stand well enough on one leg for me to button her into a dress. Then I would maneuver the wheelchair behind her, she would plop down,

I would lift her feet onto the footrests and make sure her left arm wasn't dangling. And we were off.

Outside, near the entrance to the three-story building, a small fenced patio contained concrete tables and benches. It was shaded by young live oak trees. We went there to sit and talk.

"Mom, does time go fast or slow for you?" I asked one day. Some of the orderlies and aides were sitting at another table, smoking on their break, and I leaned close. It seemed to me a private question.

"What do you mean?" She looked at me with pleasant curiosity. A breeze stirred the leaves above us and lifted a few strands of white hair off her forehead. Her light blue sweater was draped over her left shoulder; I had managed to get only her right arm into its sleeve.

"In your head. What goes through your head? Do you think about time passing?" Or, I wondered, did time not exist except as hunger or discomfort? I tried to imagine the effort of finding sense in her confusion. Was it like trying to hear a single drop of water falling in Niagara Falls?

Maybe it was easier to find no sense, to let the roar fill everything.

She struggled for the meaning of the question, her face distressed with thought. "I remember things," she said.

"Like what?"

"I remember you when you were a little boy." She smiled. "And Rusty. He rode in an inner tube when we went swimming."

Rusty was my dog, a small imitation of a Gordon setter. "Mom, that's wonderful!" I said. She had no memory for the immediate past, but by reaching back she resurrected my own memories. "Do you remember Whiskers?"

"Of course I do," she said. She paused and looked up at the side of the building. "I remember lots of things."

"Do you remember the tornado that time we went to Michigan? There was a slapping screen door. I was real little."

"That would have been . . . we must have gone to visit my family. But I don't remember a tornado."

The breeze stirred again, pushing a residue of

leaves around the patio. The employees rose and moved past us toward the patio gate. One of the women trailed a hand on Mom's shoulder. "How're you feeling today, Clare?" she said.

"Oh, fine, thank you," Mom replied.

"Because you've got your son here."

"Yes." Mom wagged her head up and down, smiling.

"Mom?" She turned her attention back to me. I said, "But how does time pass? Does it fly by? Does it drag? Do you think about it?"

She shook her head. "I don't know," she said. She looked up at the building again, to the row of third-floor windows. "It's nice here," she said. "Is that our apartment?"

I followed her gaze. "Well, kind of," I said.

"I thought so," she said. She plucked at the sweater on her shoulder. "I think I'd better go in now."

Getting her up and dressed and in the chair became more difficult. She wanted to spend more time in bed. I would read to her from the newspapers. The local paper didn't interest her after a while; it took the weird inventions of the supermarket tabloids to keep her listening, and even then sometimes she fell asleep. She developed psoriasis, which she scratched compulsively when she was awake. "Stop scratching, Mom, you'll make it worse," I told her, sounding like a mother. I recruited Dad and we would stand on each side of her, rubbing lotion on her arms and legs and neck and shoulders. We began finding her in diapers. More and more, she resisted the exercises prescribed to keep her muscles from withering completely.

The aides kept trying to make her walk. On her birthday weekend in mid-April, I watched as a stout, sympathetic woman named Willie Mae urged her from her room into the hall, half carrying her, saying, "Come on, Clare. You can't just lie there, honey, you got to get some exercise." She turned Mom toward the end of the hall and tried to make her start walking. Mom let herself go limp and sprawled in the woman's strong arms.

"Just try, Mom. You've got to keep trying," I said.

Willie Mae shifted a hip under her and began to move her down the hall. Mom slumped. She would move nothing. "Leave me alone. Leave me alone. Nick, make them stop!" she begged. A loud, piteous groan escaped her. Then she cried out, "Why don't they just let me die!" I turned away and brought her wheelchair.

A few weeks later, I was in London covering a story for a travel magazine when Barbara called to say Mom had had another stroke, and this time was in a coma.

It was hard to believe she wasn't just sleeping. She breathed softly and quickly through her mouth, and I spoke to her because I didn't know what else to do. I told her Dad was in the hospital, too.

I had entered the apartment as I always did to find Dad in his accustomed position on the couch, dressed as usual in his khakis and thread-bare, strap-shouldered undershirt, and as usual he had looked up from his crossword and broken into a smile. He stood up, hopped, and rubbed his thigh. We went out to lunch, and he walked with a different limp.

"It's been bothering me," he said. "Arthritis."

"Let's get you checked," I said. I was surprised when he agreed. He must have been worried. Last year he'd resisted going to the doctor. "I'm fine," he'd said at the time, and the general checkup I'd finally gotten him to go for proved uneventful. Nothing obvious had changed since then. His pacemaker ticked along, he still was a breakfast regular at Woolworth's, and he still coveted the seat next to Bess when he could catch a ride. Otherwise he kept to himself. He refused to wear his hearing aid or go to the senior day care center, where he might have been able to draw or paint a little. Over the months, I had started seeing more candy and fewer staples in his refrigerator. He stopped swimming. Some new videotapes, all cartoons, appeared on the television stand. I began to find small toys here and there in the apartment. His Gibbon and his Manchester lay unopened, evidence of a forlorn lassitude. Next to that, this new limp seemed innocuous.

"It's my arthritis," Dad said preemptively as we entered the doctor's examining room.

The doctor pressed the top of the right upper leg where Dad said it hurt. Dad winced and drew in breath. The doctor probed and poked at him some more, then sent me off with him for blood tests. The next day he called to tell me he wanted to admit Dad to the hospital. Dad sat glumly while I completed the admission papers. And soon after that, a CAT scan revealed the metastatic cancer glowing in his bones like phosphorescence. It had originated in his prostate. Now it was in his shoulders, ribs, back, and legs.

Dad was sitting in bed in a bright room on an upper floor of Lee Memorial Hospital. The setting was deliberately cheerful; keeping doubts at bay was important in the diagnostic wing. I walked to the window and looked down at a vivid X that marked a helicopter pad. A quarter-mile away, white against the Florida green, the buildings of the high school I'd attended twenty-seven years earlier glimmered in the sun.

"They think it's cancer, Dad," I said.

"They'll take care of it, though, won't they?" he said. He asked the question as if he wanted assurances instead of knowledge. His forehead glistened with some kind of ointment. It was clearer than it had been in months.

"They say there are a few things they can do. One thing is . . ." I leaned close and said into his ear, "They can remove your testicles."

He looked at me as if I were joking. "My testicles?" He was ready to laugh.

"They think testosterone feeds the cancer. Removing the source is supposed to help. But I suppose you're attached to them."

He smiled wanly. "Yes," he said. "I think I'll keep them. I don't want any surgery." He shook his head emphatically.

There was little more that could be done. He started a series of estrogen injections, which were supposed to counteract the "feeding" effect of the testosterone. A few days later the doctor, a tall, bland young man who'd found a level of removed concern, said gravely that he was discharging Dad "to keep from using up his Medicare." With no alternative, I took him home. "I'll be fine," he said, but he was weak, and he clung to my arm as we entered the apartment. I settled him down for a nap, checked the refrigerator, and left for the airport, forcing myself to believe he'd be okay.

Barbara and I had just gone to bed, around midnight, when the phone rang. It was Bess. "It's your dad, honey," she said. "He's back in the hospital, poor thing." She had checked on him and called an ambulance when she found him still in bed, semiconscious, the sheets and pillows soaked with blood. Blood? My God, I'd seen no sign of blood. I wouldn't have left him if I had. I couldn't imagine what had broken loose; was it one of the lesions in his forehead, a hemorrhoidal artery, or something else? I never learned. But I had to acknowledge, in a wave of guilt, that I had been too quick to leave him, to leave behind the weight of his infirmity.

He wasn't discharged this time. When I made my daily call a few days later, the operator switched me to oncology, the cancer ward.

Oncology was dark and quiet compared with the diagnostic wing. There was a hush about it, the held breath of waiting. Barbara and I walked down a hall into a cul-de-sac of rooms set around a central nursing station. Dad's room was at ten o'clock. We found him sitting up in bed, staring toward a window that this time gave no long view but looked upon the beige brick wall of a hospital wing under construction.

A smile broke across his face when he saw us, dazzling me once again with his transformation from unhappiness to bright fulfillment. "Hi,

Nick. What's the score?" he said. "When am I going to get out of here?"

"I don't know, Dad," I said. "I have to talk to the doctors."

"I hope it's soon," he said. "I'm ready to go home."

"I'll bet you are."

"What's happened with your mother, anyway?" he demanded.

Mom remained in a coma. She had been returned to the nursing home, where she lay curled up like an aged fetus, fed by a tube in her stomach. If it were left to her, I doubt she would have gone for it. Her living will said she didn't want to be kept alive by extraordinary means. We had told the hospital and both nursing homes that she didn't want resuscitation, and now we asked about the feeding tube. The nursing home explained that in Florida, "extraordinary" meant machines like respirators, but the law required feeding her even if it meant a tube into her stomach.

Dad stared out the window for a long moment when I told him this. He looked back and shook his head. "I don't know, Nick," he said.

Barbara said, "Let's worry about you, Jack. You'd better get up and let us help you walk around. You don't want to forget how."

We got him up and into a pair of slippers, and with one of us on each side of him, we walked him around the nurses' station. He clung to us, muscles quivering, dragging his feet. I could hardly believe how quickly he had gone from walking to this tortured shuffling. Each step took an enormous effort. We reached the door of his room and he veered toward it. We tried to steer him on a second circuit and he said no. He fell back on the bed, looking haggard. "I guess it's going to be a long road for me," he said.

"Long road for what?" I asked.

"Till I get any peace and comfort."

We spent the next week shuttling between the hospital and the nursing home, which was practically next door. Mom lay there, eyelids flickering, lips crusted, hair mussed by the pillow, breathing into eternity. I would hold her hand and talk to her, kiss her on the cheek on leaving, and I knew that somehow she perceived what we felt for her.

Barbara and I were rushing, as usual, the day we were to return to New York. We stopped at my parents' bank and she waited in the car while I hurried in to do some business. She was sitting with the door open, reading, when I dashed out again. It was not before we reached the hospital and started to get out of the car that she realized one of her sandals was missing. We returned and found it in the parking lot, then hurried back to complete our visits.

Barbara and I stood beside Mom's bed, leaned on the side rail that she was no longer able to object to, and told her the story of the missing sandal. It sounded scatterbrained and silly, and we laughed in the telling. Mom's eyelids flickered as if her eyes were darting under the closed lids, as the eyes of dreamers do. Suddenly her eyes popped open and seemed to scan the ceiling. My heart froze. "Mom," I said. "Mom!"

But part of me, even as I responded, didn't want her to wake up again. What was the point? What would be the point of dragging her exhausted body through more pain while I dredged her mind for its few lucid kernels? This was not my mother. This was not the woman she had been, nor the woman she would have wanted to be. I was grateful for her life. But it had ceased to be the full thing that it had been, and I was ready to let go of her.

Her eyes raked the ceiling. The lids fluttered and closed. I squeezed her hand and kissed her. As we left, the woman in the bed nearest the door said, "It's very nice the way you treat your mother."

We were back home in New York that night when the phone woke us after midnight. It was the nursing home, calling to say that she had died.

"Dad?" I entered the room quietly, Barbara following. He was staring at the window. He jerked his head toward me, and the smile was absent, replaced by the dragging weight of time. He seemed both surprised and, in an instant, apprehensive. "Mom died early yesterday," I said.

He gave a ragged sigh and turned back to the window.

"She died in her sleep," I said. "It was the best thing."

"I'm going to miss her," he said.

"I know. So will I."

We arranged a small memorial service two

days later. I expected Dad would come. I had told him about it and asked the oncology nurses to help get him ready. The duty nurse called that morning. "Your father doesn't think he can make it," she said. "He says he just doesn't feel up to it."

Nothing I said could change his mind. A small group gathered at the church that soft June morning. I was brave. I didn't cry, although I thought I would. I quoted Jorge Amado, which she would have liked, from a sweet story called "The Swallow and the Tom Cat": "We all know how Time rushes by when we're happy. The truth is, Time never does what we want him to. When you beg him to linger awhile, he runs away as fast as he can and before you know it the happy days are gone. When you want him to fly away faster than a thought because you're unhappy or going through a bad time, you can't get rid of him and the hours creep by." I said I thought time was passing very quickly for my mother now.

Dad replaced her in the nursing home. He never thought it would be permanent. In mid-July, he began a letter to a couple who had written after seeing Mom's obituary: "Certainly glad to get your letter. Sad to say that Clare left us some time ago. Since, I have been rattling around in the Lee Convalescent Center. Not too bad. I have a comfortable bed and room and the food is O.K. Nick and I will be moving into an apartment pretty soon, as soon as he gets things squared away. But of course I miss Clare more than anything. She just stopped breathing one night."

He apparently could go no further. He started the letter twice and stopped it there each time. I had said nothing to make him believe we were moving into an apartment. Wishful thinking was at work. And something more, perhaps: a desperate, powerful rejection of the ironic circle that seemed to be closing in his life, shunted away as a child and again, as he must have seen it, as an old man, again left to the kindness of strangers.

I arrived on a Saturday morning in August to find him sitting in his wheelchair in the lobby, angled between a sofa and a plastic plant, crossword in his lap, alone, as he seemed to prefer. He looked up and unfurled his lovely smile. "What's the score, Nick?" he asked. "When am I going to go home?"

Each time before I'd told the efficacious lie:

"Dad, you have to keep walking, get a little stronger, keep taking the estrogen. Then we'll see." As a result, he had haunted the nursing home's social worker since June, arguing that he was ready to leave. This time I suggested we go to the apartment after we'd had breakfast.

The summer heat met us at the door as we left the nursing home. Dad opened it with a foot as I pushed him through. It was as efficient a collaboration as we'd managed to achieve in life, a simple marriage of abilities toward a common need, stripped at last of attitude. I felt for a happy second as if we should go around opening doors all over town. I wheeled him to the curb and helped him into the car; the chair was a permanent fixture now. At first he'd been able to walk with my help and we'd been able to leave it behind. But edema had swollen his feet and ankles, and walking was impossible. He wore a catheter all the time as well.

The morning sky was clear of the thunderheads that would gather later in the day at this time of year. I drove the long way, through the posh old neighborhood that paralleled the river, past Thomas Edison's winter home, where even in the heat of August tourists were waiting at the crosswalk, and into the asphalt clearing of the shopping center.

Woolworth's lunch counter held its group of regulars. They looked up as we entered, and in the instant it took their eyes to flicker between me and Dad, I saw pity mingle with their welcomes. Later, when we left, I saw heads together, talking. They weren't gossiping about my father. I think they feared for him, and for themselves as well. He had changed so much in so short a time that he reminded them of their mortality.

The chair's wheels sank into the carpet as we entered the apartment. He couldn't push himself with his arms or scoot the chair along. I maneuvered him around the dining table to the window. He leaned forward and looked out. Distant clouds smudged the horizon. The trap-tending fisherman was shuttling between his marker buoys, a cloud of gray-and-white gulls trailing the boat. A ketch sailed upriver on a broad reach. I handed Dad the binoculars he kept near the window, but he shook his head and pulled back from the window.

"Now what?" he said.

"I paid some bills," I said. "There were—"

"It doesn't matter, Nick," he said. "If I can't trust you, who can I trust?"

I wheeled him into the bedroom so he could assure himself that everything was just as he had left it, waiting for him to come home. He lifted a hand from the chair arm and motioned at the dresser. "In the drawer . . . ," he said.

"You want something out of there?" I opened the upper lefthand drawer, the one in which he kept his wallet, money, his defining odds and ends, such as penknives, passport, some wood and bone pins he'd carved after pre-Columbian forms, and a plastic box that contained jewelry I'd never seen him wear. He'd given me a pair of thin gold cufflinks from it years before.

"That," he said, reaching for the box.

I handed it to him. He opened it and peered inside, then scuffled through old coins and buttons and brought out a thick gold chain. He scuffled some more and produced an ornate pocket watch. He looked up with pride and satisfaction. "My father's watch and chain," he said. He held them out to me.

The chain was heavy. I let it fall upon itself into my hand until the links gleamed dully in a mound the size of a small stone. The watch, too, had an authoritative weight. Its stem was frozen from either overwinding or neglect, but with the chain and its elaborate decoration it had been the mark of a man's substance. Dad said, "You should have this."

"Are you sure?" I said.

He nodded. "It was your grandfather's."

"Thanks, Dad," I said. I returned the chain and watch to the box with the buttons and coins. "I'll leave it here until you come home, in case you need it."

"Well . . . ," he said, hesitating. He had always been possessive with his things. "But I don't think I'm going to be needing it."

We left the apartment and drove across the bridge that arched high over the wide river. We ate lunch at a restaurant that looked out on a marina. Later, when I left him at the nursing home, he said, "I miss her. I wish you lived closer."

"I do, too, Dad," I said. Barbara and I had talked about moving him to a nursing home in New York, and asked him if he would like that. He said no. He would have been no less miserable. As it was, I was relatively undistracted during the time I spent with him. My time was his, so I didn't mind kneeling behind his chair to hook and unhook the discreet blue envelope that held his catheter bag, for example, or wrestling the chair in and out of the car trunk. I regarded him tenderly.

Those brief times were all I had to give him. I picked him up the next day and asked him what he'd like for lunch. All summer, after years of ordering from the cheap side of the menu, he had indulged a taste for lobster. This time the mention of lunch brought the usual look of expectation to his face, but he groped for words. "I'd like one of those . . . one of those . . . one of those fishy things." There was nothing on any menu that would kill him at that point. We ordered Bloody Marys and broiled lobster tails. He chose the Mississippi mud pie for dessert. He reduced the slab of chocolate to crumbs, dabbed at his mouth with a napkin, and said, "That was good." He wore a ravished look, a vampiric sated sickness.

We went from lunch to the Edison Mall, bought the Sunday *New York Times* and a magazine in which I had an article, and chose a spot to read and people-watch. He had to go to the bathroom. I wheeled him in and waited outside the stall until he finished. We went to a department store, where I bought him some new underwear. We stopped at a store window to look at some knives that he admired, perused the bookstores, looked at some fishing rods and tennis rackets, killing time. We returned to the car finally, where I unstrung his apparatus and maneuvered him into the seat. As I was climbing behind the wheel, he said, "We could go to Edison Mall, couldn't we?"

"We just left Edison Mall," I said.

He looked surprised and disappointed.

That night, after I dropped him at the nursing home, I unwrapped the underwear I'd bought him and printed his name in black block letters with a laundry marker on each item. I left it with him the next day on my way to the airport.

Jerry Chambers's father died that month. It had been eight years since his paralyzing stroke and three since he had become "unresponsive," a gray and neutral word for living death. Jerry had been able only to surmise that his father recognized him during those three years. Still, he told me, "I wish I'd been there when he died."

His mother, increasingly frail but adamantly independent, remained at the mountain farmhouse to which she'd returned almost two years earlier for the fall display of colors. Jerry had the dubious solace, between his visits, of knowing that the county sheriff drove by from time to time to check on her.

The cancer was moving quickly in my father. I planned to see him again for his birthday, in October, on Columbus Day. Bess hesitated when I told her. "Well, honey, I don't know," she said. "He's not doing real well. You might should come a little sooner." I moved my schedule up two weeks. Bess mused on this, a weighted "Hmmm." When I called the nursing home to check on his condition, the head nurse on his floor said, "You'd better come now."

I arrived at eleven on a Sunday night, September 23. The nursing home was locked. I rapped on the glass front door until a figure appeared in an outpost of light at the end of the long hall. The figure motioned me toward a side door. When I reached the door, one of the night nurses peered out at me, suspicious of this late visitation. I said, "I'm John Taylor's son."

She led me down the corridor, which seemed eerily quiet without the television, the conversations, the various rustlings of the waking hours. Past the nursing station in the hall leading to the front entrance, the door to my father's room was open and a light was on.

The scene from the doorway was like the pieta, the supine Christ in the arms of Mary, except that my father had not achieved the peace of death. He labored and was in pain. A nurse by his shoulder said, "John. John, your son is here," and helped him as he struggled to sit up. So ingrained in us were the niceties that he smiled as best he could and croaked my name, and I, chipper in response, said, "Hi, Dad. How are you feeling?" The instant I said it I felt like an idiot. He was dying, and yet habit or denial or fool's hope would not let us deal with that. The specter loomed, and we pretended that it wasn't there.

The nurse knew more than I. When I told her to let him sleep, she said, "Are you sure?" And I said yes, because he was struggling so. Sleep would renew him. Tomorrow would be different.

We could talk then. But I would never talk with him again.

You would think death would be more physically dramatic than it is, but Erasmus had it pegged. It is the passage toward death that provides the drama, that is harder and more painful than death itself. Dad struggled all the next day as I sat at his bedside. Nurses and orderlies came to turn him, clean him, change his bedding, inject him against the pain. He howled in agony each time they had to move him, then subsided to rasping, trembling quietude.

Toward the end of the day the attendants withdrew, as if some signal had passed among them. Dad's breathing grew steadily more shallow. I placed my hand over his and waited. Each drawn breath and exhalation took more time than the last. Each was weaker, a flutter of a bird's wing. I struggled with myself, not wanting him to die but praying that he be released. And then he simply didn't breathe again. His features softened and relaxed. After a long, suspended moment I stood up, kissed him on the forehead, said "I love you" to his body, and went to find a nurse.

She came into the room and placed a stethoscope against his chest. "That's funny," she said. "Usually the pacemakers keep working. His stopped."

I walked out of the nursing home that September night an orphan. It was some time before I took the measure of what had happened to me. I had been thinking about my parents' deaths for so long that the anticipation had become second nature. Now that it had happened, I was lost. For a time I found it almost impossible to work. Perhaps Mom had known this would happen when she wrote their obituaries all those years ago, for the days just after their deaths were made easier by having them at hand.

1991

The year turned before I cleared their personal things from the apartment and put it up for sale. And it was that November before I was prepared for dealing with their ashes. I had resisted the memorial urns and fancy boxes pressed on me by the cremation society; my parents would have scoffed at them. But they would have liked to be in a place they thought of fondly. So Barbara and I rented a sailboat on the day after Thanksgiving and sailed on a brisk breeze from the mouth of the Caloosahatchee River into the Gulf of Mexico. We had with us the boxes of ashes and some red hibiscus and purple oleander blossoms we'd picked along the roadside. We reached along Fort Myers Beach to a spot near the south end, well

offshore from the beach where Mom and Dad had taken me swimming and the dog Rusty had ridden in the inner tube. There I sprinkled the ashes and tossed the flowers after them and said a prayer.

We came about and ambled back up the island's length. There were sails on the horizon and a rainbow far off, and it all seemed so perfect, and we were so relieved to be alive that we made love in the cockpit of the boat as we sailed away from the pale stain of the ashes.

How, then, do I remember them without a gravestone or some other marker to attend? The watch and chain my father gave me were stolen in a burglary. I have photographs and letters. I miss my parents' letters. I miss writing to them, for from no one else could I expect such unqualified approval. I have my father's prints and tools and the childhood memoirs I asked them both to write. I have memories. Most of all, I have myself. Me. I am what my parents made and left. I am what I have to remember them by. And I am the person that they made. I will have to do with that, but all in all, it's not so bad.

A woman friend of mine, after learning that

they had died, asked, "So how do you feel now? Guilty? Inadequate?"

No doubt she was well-meaning, but the question astounded me with its acceptance of guilt as a condition of living. I felt sad. I didn't know then how much I would miss them. But I didn't feel guilty or inadequate. They died knowing that I loved them. I always knew that they loved me. We had cared for each other as best we could, while caring for ourselves. There is really nothing more to know that matters.